Also by Arthur

The Simplest Path to Wealth: Turn $50,000 into $3.3 Million

Stop Paying Your Credit Cards: Obtain Credit Card Debt Forgiveness Vol 1

Debt Forgiveness, Volume 2 When Creditors Decide to Sue

Dynamic Budgeting Techniques: Cut your expenses in half and double your income

How Much Federal Income Tax Will I Pay in 2018? The New Tax Law's winners and losers

Living Rich & Loving It: Your guide to a rich, happy, healthy, simple and balanced life

DISCLAIMER

The Six Million Dollar Retiree:

Your roadmap to a six million dollar retirement nest egg

Arthur V. Prosper

 * A-TEAM PUBLISHING GROUP * PO BOX 153 * PINEBROOK, NEW JERSEY 07058

PAPERBACK ISBN: 9781980234456
Imprint: Independently published by:
A-Team, PO Box 153, Pinebrook, NJ 07058
Cover Design by: Kristjan Victorino
Printed in the United States
Author's Email Address: arthurvprosper@gmail.com

ABOUT THE AUTHOR

Arthur V. Prosper heads the finance department of a privately held manufacturing firm in the great state of New Jersey. Previously, he was the Vice President of Finance of the Kuoni Group and the Accounting Director of Cantel Medical. He was responsible for the financial objectives, retirement and benefit plans, investment goals and capital structures of the companies he worked for.

Arthur V. Prosper is a freelance writer, author and columnist with 30 years of market experience. He writes articles about the markets and finance under the header "DidoSphere, DidoSpin and Vox Populi". He is the author of several published articles in business, politics, sports and entertainment including: How We Got Here, Market Crash of 2008, Housing Bubble, The Obama Recession, Bank Stress Tests & Other Terms, Scrap Mark to Market Valuation, Recession Over, The Labyrinth of Obamacare, Bush-Obama Recession, No Different From the Rest, A Tale of Two States, NJ & VA, SEC's Case vs. GS&CO., Weak, Most Experts Agree, PIIGS: Too Big to Fail, What Causes Stock Market Fluctuations, Sluggish Recovery, Good for Investors, QE2=Printing Money, Stock Market Investors, Fasten Your Seatbelt, No Double Dip Recession, 10% Unemployment Rate, Not Enough to Derail Recovery

Table of Contents

Introduction 1

PART I – Your path towards six million dollars 7

Make at least $5000 a month gross salary 9

Save at least $1000 a month – Should you convert to a Roth IRA/401k or not? 11

Earn at least 10% APY (annual percentage yield) on your savings 20

Asset allocation for a minimum 10% annual return 27

Purchase Your Primary Residence 29

Collect Social Security benefits at the right time 39

PART II – How to save at least $1000 a month 44

Get Rid of All Your Consumer Debts 44

Reduce Your Taxes 46

Reduce life, disability, health, auto and homeowner's insurance 51

Enroll in a H.S.A. (Health Savings Accounts) 52

Reduce your children's college costs 54

Avoid Conspicuous Consumption 58

Shop Around for Everything 60

Do not pay off your mortgage - Good Debt, Bad Debt 61

How to make 10% APR on borrowed money 65

Do not save for an Emergency Fund – there are better ways of dealing with emergencies 67

Stop Wasting Food, Energy, Natural Resources 69

If You Have a Pet, You Must Read This 70

PART III - Never Lose any of Your Savings 71

Don't focus on taxes - Tax on retirement income, not a big deal 71

Never Buy an Investment Property 76

Double Taxation on 401k Loans? 77

Do not invest in anything you don't understand 78

Do Not Take Unnecessary Risks, Don't Do Anything Stupid..... 79

PART IV – Protect your six million dollar pot of Gold 83

Estate Planning, asset protection - Setting up a trust to avoid probate, exposure to creditors and predators 84

Insurance Policy vs. IRA, which is better for your heirs? How to protect RMDs from taxation 89

Paying for Long-Term Care.. 98

My LTC Strategy.. 107

How to reduce income to qualify for Medicaid 114

Creative Ways of Hiding Assets to Qualify for Medicaid 115

Other Retirement Ideas.. 121

Annuities, what are they?.. 132

Retiring within 10 years 138

Retiring within 5 years... 138

Other investments before and during retirement...................... 139

Investing in retirement & required minimum distribution (RMD)... 140

Where to Invest Your Excess RMD.. 146

Enrich Your Life by Exploring the World.................. 147

Staying Healthy and Fit as You Age 149

How does the new tax law affect the retirement strategies in this book? 154

Conclusion.. 155

Living Rich & Loving It.. 157

Excerpt from the book, Living Rich & Loving It: 159

Supplemental Disclaimer... 160

Introduction

I want to thank you for purchasing this book. If this book is worthy of your praise, your positive review would be much appreciated.

How much money do you need to retire? Conventional wisdom has it that saving a million dollars for retirement is the magic number that will give most retirees security and peace of mind in retirement. A rule of thumb that many financial planners apply is a formula of 20 to 25 x annual gross salary. For example, $60,000 annual salary x 20 = $1,200,000 is the minimum target amount you will need to provide you with financial independence in retirement so that you will live off the interest of your savings and never touch the principal. In a survey conducted by financial planner, *Wes Moss of Capital Investment Advisors in Atlanta*, he discovered that most people would be happy in retirement with savings of about $500,000. So why is this book entitled, ***"The Six Million Dollar Retiree",*** whose main goal is to teach readers how to save, not half a million, not a million dollars, but 6 million dollars for retirement? Because, 1) Setting a goal of saving 6 million dollars for retirement is a realistic and achievable goal and this book will show you how to do it, 2) A million dollars isn't what it used to be, 3) This amount of savings will serve as your safety net for catastrophic events and life changes such as major illnesses, loss of income, lawsuits, disability, divorce, depression, mid-life crises, death of a partner, long-term care expenses, being a crime victim, accidents, market losses, inflation, recessions, health insurance increases and drastic changes in the tax system, 4) this amount of money will allow you to leave a lasting legacy for generations to come, and finally, 5) Aiming high towards a six million dollar retirement nest egg will help you develop budgeting and investing skills and prudent savings and spending habits which you will most likely pass on to your children and grandchildren.

Although money may not be enough to insulate you from all the unexpected downturns and tumbles in life, having enough money will cushion the fall. If you strive for six million dollars and you only hit 1, 2 or 3 million dollars, you are way ahead of the game. Money helps buy safety, convenience, freedom and luxury. Money will help you create hopes and dreams in your retirement to keep you young at heart. Money will make it easier for you to create enjoyable moments for yourself and loved ones so that you will always have something to look forward to which is the key to happiness.

My objective for writing this book is to touch and improve the quality of life of everyone who reads it. I am hoping that the reader will put the life-changing ideas presented in this book into practice. Since there is no "one size fits all" when it comes to retirement planning, the purpose of this book is NOT to convince you to take my personal preferences as gospel, but rather to educate you of the various options available to you so you may judge, reason and analyze my opinions and the facts as they apply to you. Throughout the book, I make it clear whether a certain subject, passage or statement is fact or my personal opinion. When necessary, I reference the source of any factual information. Various advice in this book do not take into consideration your age, health, objectives, financial situation or needs. Before acting on any advice, you should consider its appropriateness and its applicability to your current situation. But the knowledge you will gain from this book should give you sufficient knowledge so as to analyze your personal situation and to empower you to ask the right questions from financial professionals, insurance brokers, lawyers and other professionals who are offering their services.

The road to a successful retirement does not have to be a rough road. You can achieve retirement success by targeting four specific goals: 1) take care of your physical and mental health as you age, 2) set a goal for you and your spouse to save $6 million dollars for retirement, 3) never lose any of the money you save and, 4) preserve your assets for your beneficiaries. It is the aim of this book to help you accomplish these goals. This book has something for you whether you have millions of dollars in assets or are struggling to get by, living paycheck to paycheck. Success means different things to different people. An extra $1000 a month in retirement is considered success for some, but for others protecting a six million dollar estate from taxation is their definition of success. Health comes first and everything else second, but lack of financial independence in retirement will cause anxiety and emotional distress which can lead to depression and a weakened immune system. Your financial health in retirement is a big factor for your physical and mental well-being. You should have the same amount of financial security in retirement as you do before retirement. You should not enter your retirement years living with financial anxiety. Your state of mind can affect your decisions. A happy and healthy retirement should mean never having to worry about how to pay for your prescriptions, health care, housing and basic necessities. Most people know the changes they want to make in retirement so they have a good idea of the amount of income they will need for their living expenses, health care, entertainment and incidental expenses. But you should strive to receive at least the same amount of income in retirement as you were receiving when you were working so as to give you more flexibility with your travel and entertainment plans and unexpected expenses and allow you to live the lifestyle you want to live.

Important topics in this book:

- **How to accumulate more than six million dollars in your pot of gold, i.e. retirement account.**

- **Comparing Life insurance vs. IRA for preservation of your assets for your heirs. The answer will surprise you.**

- **Debunking the greatest tax myth of all: "Your million dollar retirement savings bumps you into a higher tax bracket so you will be paying 40 cents on the dollar". See chapter, "Don't Focus on Taxes – Tax on Retirement Income Not a Big Deal"**

- **How to determine if converting to a Roth IRA or Roth 401k is right for you. Ed Slott, the IRA guru says converting your IRA to a Roth IRA is tantamount to moving your account from "accounts that are forever taxed to accounts that are never taxed". WRONG! See Chapter, "Save at Least $1000 a Month..."**

- **How to allocate your assets correctly and diversify based on your risk tolerance level.**

- **Avoiding Veblen Goods – the savings will amaze you.**

- **Shop around for everything. If you are struggling to make ends meet, this chapter will show you why. Learn how to save more and spend less.**

- **Purchasing your primary residence – Pros and cons of owning vs. renting. The analysis chart shows the clear winner which will surprise you.**

- **How to distinguish good debt from bad debt---when borrowing makes sense. Analysis table proves that some debts are good.**

- **Never take unnecessary risks. Don't do anything stupid. This chapter shows that stupidity is the great equalizer in life. Doing any of the things on the list may change your life or worse end it in the blink of an eye.**

- **Stay away from rental properties. This chapter tells you why it is not worth being an absentee landlord.**

- **How to handle emergencies without an emergency fund. The analysis chart shows how much money you will save by not having an emergency fund. The figures will astound you.**

This chapter also shows the reader where to get cash for emergencies once you get rid of your emergency fund.

- **Never ever listen to Suze Orman that 401k loans are taxed twice. 401k loans are not taxed twice. This chapter proves it.**

- **How to maximize your Social Security benefits – In light of the elimination of "File and Suspend" and "Restricted Application" strategies, the chart shows claiming strategies for 1) Single never married, 2) currently married, 3) married at least 10 years, divorced at least 2 years, currently single, 4) divorced, has remarried and currently married, 5) widow/widower, 6) surviving divorced spouse, married at least 10 years, currently single or remarried after the age of 60.**

- **Finding the best places for retirement – Some of these retirement communities are surprising. Some viable locations have ½ the cost of living of many U.S. cities. But should you pack your bags and move there now? Find out in this chapter.**

- **Paying for nursing home and long-term care. The cost of nursing home and long term care can wipe out your entire estate. Read this chapter for solutions.**

- **How to qualify for Medicaid benefits for LTC. You do not have to spend down your savings. This chapter explains many different ways some retirees have been dealing with the "spend down" dilemma.**

- **Estate planning. How to skip probate, minimize your taxes and protect your estate from frivolous law suits and creditor claims.**

- **How to enrich your life by exploring the world – Travel as soon as you can while you are still young. This chapter discusses why the money you spend traveling and exploring the world is money well spent.**

- **Staying Healthy and Fit as You Age – There are a few minor behavior modification changes that you can put into practice that will keep you healthy throughout your retirement years.**

****

PART I – Your path towards six million dollars

The following 30-year chart shows how you will reach your goal of saving six million dollars for retirement. The figures shown are not adjusted for inflation. If you save six million dollars, inflation will be of little consequence. As inflation goes up, so will interest rates and the value of stocks. (Source: http://www.investopedia.com/university/inflation/inflation4.asp)

Your investments should be earning more as the rate of inflation rises. If you begin your savings program at 37 years old, you will have 30 years to build up your savings before full retirement age of 67 (FRA for persons born 1960 and later). But even if you only have 10 years to save before retirement, and even if you only earn the median household income of $56,500 (Source: US CENSUS BUREAU) you can still save more than $1 million dollars for retirement if you follow the strategies shown in this book. See additional charts in Part II and III. The rationale for a 30-year chart is to provide an allowance for child rearing years. Raising children is expensive and to be conservative, we will assume that you and your wife will only start this savings program at age 37.

CHART 1	
START YOUR 30 YEAR SAVINGS PROGRAM TODAY:	
Employee Monthly	
contribution to deferred	
retirement account	
(401K, 403B, 457B)	1,000
Growth of your	
account after	
30 years at 10%	
APY (Annual Yield)	2,260,469
Employer Safe Harbor	
Match (Estimated)	
Approx. 27% of	
Employee contribution	
= $270 per month	
Growth of company	
match after 30 years	
at 10% APY	610,327
BALANCE AFTER 30 YEARS	2,870,795
SPOUSE'S ACCOUNT	2,870,795
RETIREMENT SAVINGS	5,741,590
EQUITY IN YOUR	
PRINCIPAL RESIDENCE	
AFTER 30 YEARS	300,000
TOTAL RETIREMENT NEST EGG	$6,041,590
Estimated Lump Sum Value of Your SS Benefits at FRA (full retirement age, Source: www.forbes.com):	
Married Couples	900,000
PROJECTED RETIREMENT ASSETS	$6,941,590

Make at least $5000 a month gross salary

You and your spouse should earn at least a combine gross annual household income of $120,000 and contribute at least 20% of the gross salary to your retirement accounts. If your household income is less, you will save less but you will still end up a millionaire by the time you retire if you follow the strategy in this book.

If your household income is less than $120,000 per annum, think of ways to increase your income to make six million dollars a realistic goal. You may have to change careers, go back to school to learn new skills so you can earn more money. If this is out of the question but you can spare 5 to 20 hours a week, why not make extra money in your spare time doing what you love? If you like driving maybe you can sign up to be an Uber and Lyft driver. If you are handy, advertise in your local newspaper for your services as a "handyman for hire". Do you enjoy yard work? Part time landscapers and gardeners are in demand and there aren't enough of them. If you don't mind doing a little dirty work, there are many offices that need cleaning after office hours. It is hard to get workers to do these odd jobs. There are hundreds of other ways you can make money in your spare time such as: Computer Repair Technician, Basic Computer Skills Instructor, Tax Preparation Service, Social Events Organizer, Seminar and Workshop Organizer/Presenter in the fields of Sports, Religion, Politics, the Economy, Real Estate Investing, Cooking and Baking, Dance Lessons, Cigar Rolling, Magic Tricks, Self Defense Techniques, Public Speaking, Make Up Demo, Couponing, Time Management, Carpentry, Painting, Drawing and Designing, Flower Arrangement, Bonsai Planting, Teaching Etiquette, Casino Gambling Tricks, Interior Design, Conducting IQ Tests, teaching a musical instrument, Positive Thinking, Poetry Reading, How to Hula Hoop, Chanting, Memory Enhancement, Voice Lessons, Acting Lessons, Chess Tactics, Karaoke Parties, Stand-up Comedy, Breathing Technique, Fitness Tricks, Resume Writing, and many many more, too many to mention. There must be something you are good at. Conducting seminars and workshops on something you enjoy doing is a great way to make extra money. Details on how to monetize some of these ideas are shown in my book, ***Dynamic Budgeting Techniques ("DynBudgTech")*** https://www.amazon.com/Dynamic-Budgeting-Techniques-expenses-double-ebook/dp/B01LZA9O3W/ref=sr_1_6?s=digital-text&ie=UTF8&qid=1499702317&sr=1-6&keywords=Arthur V. Prosper

There are many other money making ideas in the above-mentioned book that may be up your alley such as, becoming a personal trainer/coach, walking tour guide, dog walking/dog sitting service, house sitting, cross country driver, GSA (government) contractor, selling autographed books, selling ads on restaurant placemats, mock interviewer, selling tiny houses, etc., etc. etc.

Save at least $1000 a month – Should you convert to a Roth IRA/401k or not?

Nowadays, saving $1000 a month does not present a hardship to many people. But perhaps many people do not realize that saving $1000 a month is all it takes to acquire financial independence in retirement. Many people casually find ways to spend any extra money they have instead of saving it. There are many people who contribute very little into their retirement accounts but drive a brand new car every three years. If this is you, why?

A discussion on Roth vs. Traditional IRA/401k is included in this chapter because the deferred tax and the interest it will earn until you retire is a big factor in the strategy presented in this book. Analysis of these two retirement plans is shown towards the end of this chapter.

Pay yourself first. Make this your first priority. Do not be like others who only save what is left over after paying all the bills. Contribute 15% to 20% of your gross income to your retirement account. Many people are managing to save more, sometimes up to 50% of their gross income (Sources: http://www.cnbc.com/2017/06/30/how-to-save-30-percent-of-your-monthly-income.html

https://www.tiaa.org/public/offer/insights/starting-out/how-much-of-my-income-should-i-save-every-month)

If your employer offers a qualified retirement plan such as a 401k, 403b or 457b it is important to contribute the maximum amount allowed by your plan. Check with your plan administrator if you can contribute the IRS maximum amount ($18,000 in 2016 plus $6000 catch up for those 50 years old and older). Check out the IRS website: https://www.irs.gov/uac/Newsroom/IRS-Announces-2016-Pension-Plan-Limitations%3B-401(k)-Contribution-Limit-Remains-Unchanged-at-$18,000-for-2016

Make sure that there are no restrictions that apply to you and your company. Tax laws change and the contribution limit changes almost every year and it is prudent to always obtain verification before acting on any information obtained from this book. If your company offers both a traditional 401k and a Roth 401k and you qualify for both (there are income limits for a Roth 401k), the advice of many financial planners is to split the contributions 50/50 between the two. There has been a lot of confusion as to the real winner between a traditional 401k and a Roth 401k. The following link shows a comparison chart between the two:

https://www.irs.gov/retirement-plans/roth-comparison-chart

The main difference between these choices is that with a traditional 401k, you pay your taxes later and with a Roth 401k, you pay your taxes now. With a traditional 401k, you make contributions with pre-tax dollars, so you get a tax break up front, helping to lower your current income tax bill. Your money, both your contributions and earnings grow tax deferred until you withdraw them. At that time, withdrawals are considered to be ordinary income and you have to pay taxes at your current tax rate. (With certain exceptions, you'll also pay a 10 percent penalty if you are under 59½.) With a Roth 401k, it's basically the reverse. You make your contributions with after-tax dollars, meaning there is no upfront tax deduction. Since taxes have already been paid, withdrawals of both contributions and earnings are tax-free at age 59½, as long as you've held the account for five years. The employer's matching contributions and their earnings will always be taxable upon withdrawal since there is no facility for prepayment of taxes at the time of contribution for the employer's match. Choosing between a traditional and Roth all comes down to deciding when it's better for you to pay the taxes, now or later. And that depends a lot on what the future may look like for you.

Ed Slott, CPA who calls himself America's IRA Expert, whom many financial experts have referred to as "the number one guy in the IRA field" taped several financial advice programs on PBS. He was named "the best source for IRA advice" by The Wall Street Journal. He is an avid "Roth Lover". Here is an excerpt from one of his taped shows on The Lange Money Hour:
****

Ed Slott: ***"....like I said, to wake up and do even better planning. So, the government's going to lose all this money, not gain money, because the first thing I would tell older people, who, in the past or now, I'm still encouraging to do Roth conversions, because I believe,***

like you, that tax-free is always better, especially when you're pulling it out, to pay once and never again. I'm a big believer of that, as you know...... So, if you can start out even with a small amount growing tax-free, that means all of those earnings grow for you, as opposed to a tax-deferred IRA or 401(k). All the earnings are growing for you and Uncle Sam. In other words, you have a partner on every dollar you earn for the rest of your life. The key planning move is to get rid of your partner so you can keep it all. Who wants to share? Start as soon as you start working, the earlier you can, the younger you are, start doing Roth IRAs if your income permits, and Roth 401(k)s at work. This way, you're starting out great. I'm sixty now, so I didn't have that opportunity until 1998, and still, I didn't even have that opportunity because of income, and 2010 was the first year I was able to convert because they repealed the income eligibility limitations. Now, everybody can convert, and it does mean paying taxes now. But for younger people, they have less. They're probably in a lower bracket. It's nothing. All they're giving up is a tax deduction. And if you get the tax deduction, it sounds good upfront, but then you pay for it for the rest of your life. I'd rather, as your book says, pay it once. You won't even feel it and it's tax-free forever, because, in retirement, to me, there's nothing better than a zero percent tax rate. You can't beat a zero percent tax rate, and that's why I converted everything I could January 4th, the first business day of 2010 when the floodgates opened and the law was repealed..... I like tax-free. Anything you can do now to turn taxable money into tax free is a good move because the minute you do that, all the earnings come back to you, and you don't want to share your earnings with Uncle Sam if you don't have to. You can pay for the privilege. You know, I call it 'there's a mortgage on your IRA.' If you pay it off early, you own it, and everything it earns, you keep, and that's the best way to go into retirement. "

****

Ed Slott claims that if you convert your traditional IRA and 401k into a Roth IRA and Roth 401k, you will be converting your accounts "from accounts that are forever taxed to accounts that are never taxed. You can't beat a zero percent tax", he says. This is not a true statement. The Congressional Budget and Finance Committees employ hundreds of financial analysts and actuaries to create many different statistical charts and actuarial tables before passing any law that affects taxes. The government does not lose money in taxes on Roth IRAs no matter what Ed Slott thinks. Ed Slott is comparing apples to oranges in his calculation. For example, for the sake of a side by side comparison, you cannot say, on the traditional 401k column I will use $10,000 contribution and on the Roth 401k column I will use a $10,000 contribution plus I will add $2000 in taxes making my cash outlay $12,000. Obviously, if you do it this way the Roth 401k will win because you spent $2000 more. Of course the figures will show that you will pay more in taxes 40 years from now since you did not consider the compound interest on the additional $2000 that you did not have to pay when you made the contribution into a traditional 401k. If everything is equal, i.e. contributions, tax rates and annual returns (8% APR used on chart 2) are all the same, then the Roth IRA and Roth 401k have no advantage over the traditional IRA and 401k as the table below shows:

Chart 2

BASIC COMPARISON Traditional 401k vs. Roth 401k	TRADITIONAL Pre-Tax	ROTH After Tax @12% Rate
$8,000 PER YEAR CONTRIBUTION		
FOR 25 YEARS	200,000	176,000
Savings growth after 25 years	631,635	555,839
Less tax rate @ 12%	(75,796)	0
Your retirement savings after 25 years	$555,839	$555,839

Bottom line is that Ed is failing to consider, 1) the deferred tax benefit from a traditional IRA and 401k, 2) the compound earnings of those deferred taxes. And as discussed in the previous paragraph, the company match on Roth contributions does not have the same tax-free treatment. Only a participant's contributions are covered by the Roth rules. When a distribution is taken on Roth Accounts, the participant's contributions and the company match are separately accounted for on IRS Form 1099-R. This is why a participant's Roth contributions and their earnings are not commingled with any other money sources.

Since it is not as simple as the preceding table in real life, I went through the exercise of creating a more realistic scenario for the purpose of doing a better comparison. The following tables show a 25 year cycle for an individual who earns $60,000 during the 1st year and receives a 3% average increase every year, so that on his 25th year he is making $121,968. His annual contribution to his retirement account is 10%. We make an assumption that the contributions will earn an APR of 8%. And that the tax rate at the time of distribution is 12%.

Chart 3

TRADITIONAL 401K						
YR		ANNUAL SALARY	Marginal Tax Rate 10% to 15%	Tax Amount	10% Contribution Pre-tax	Running Bal @ 8% Annual Yield
1	$	60,000	10%	6,000	6,000	6,480
2	$	61,800	10%	6,180	6,180	13,673
3	$	63,654	10%	6,365	6,365	21,641
4	$	65,564	10%	6,556	6,556	30,453
5	$	67,531	10%	6,753	6,753	40,183
6	$	69,556	10%	6,956	6,956	50,910
7	$	71,643	10%	7,164	7,164	62,720
8	$	73,792	10%	7,379	7,379	75,707
9	$	76,006	10%	7,601	7,601	89,972
10	$	78,286	10%	7,829	7,829	105,625
11	$	80,635	12%	9,676	8,063	122,784
12	$	83,054	12%	9,966	8,305	141,576
13	$	85,546	12%	10,265	8,555	162,141
14	$	88,112	12%	10,573	8,811	184,629
15	$	90,755	12%	10,891	9,076	209,201
16	$	93,478	12%	11,217	9,348	236,032
17	$	96,282	12%	11,554	9,628	265,313
18	$	99,171	12%	11,901	9,917	297,249
19	$	102,146	15%	15,322	10,215	332,060
20	$	105,210	15%	15,782	10,521	369,988
21	$	108,367	15%	16,255	10,837	411,291
22	$	111,618	15%	16,743	11,162	456,249
23	$	114,966	15%	17,245	11,497	505,165
24	$	118,415	15%	17,762	11,842	558,367
25	$	121,968	15%	18,295	12,197	616,209
	Marginal tax rate at retirement				12%	$ (73,945)
	Retirement balance net of taxes					$ 542,264

Chart 4

YR	ROTH 401K ANNUAL SALARY	Marginal Tax Rate 10% to 15%	Tax Amount	10% Contribution Less tax	Running Bal @ 8% Annual Yield
1	$ 60,000	10%	6,000	5,400	5,832
2	$ 61,800	10%	6,180	5,562	12,306
3	$ 63,654	10%	6,365	5,729	19,477
4	$ 65,564	10%	6,556	5,901	27,408
5	$ 67,531	10%	6,753	6,078	36,165
6	$ 69,556	10%	6,956	6,260	45,819
7	$ 71,643	10%	7,164	6,448	56,448
8	$ 73,792	10%	7,379	6,641	68,136
9	$ 76,006	10%	7,601	6,841	80,975
10	$ 78,286	10%	7,829	7,046	95,063
11	$ 80,635	12%	9,676	7,096	110,331
12	$ 83,054	12%	9,966	7,309	127,051
13	$ 85,546	12%	10,265	7,528	145,345
14	$ 88,112	12%	10,573	7,754	165,347
15	$ 90,755	12%	10,891	7,986	187,200
16	$ 93,478	12%	11,217	8,226	211,061
17	$ 96,282	12%	11,554	8,473	237,096
18	$ 99,171	12%	11,901	8,727	265,489
19	$ 102,146	15%	15,322	8,682	296,105
20	$ 105,210	15%	15,782	8,943	329,452
21	$ 108,367	15%	16,255	9,211	365,756
22	$ 111,618	15%	16,743	9,488	405,263
23	$ 114,966	15%	17,245	9,772	448,238
24	$ 118,415	15%	17,762	10,065	494,968
25	$ 121,968	15%	18,295	10,367	545,762
	After tax balance				$ 545,762
	ROTH 401K WINS BY				$ 3,498

In this specific scenario, the Roth 401k wins by $3,498 after 25 years. After making other charts of different scenarios, I came to the conclusion that the only projection you have to make is your income in retirement which should show what your future tax rate would be based on the current tax system. If your retirement income will be less than your income now, traditional IRAs are better. If not, ROTH are better and you should take steps now to convert. Some retirees who do not make a correct projection of their retirement income, may be faced with an annual Required Minimum Distribution (RMD) of $100,000 or more. But so what? If you saved over $1 million for retirement, pay the tax on your withdrawals. The taxes will not be as bad as many "financial entertainers" make it out to be. See Chapter, "**Don't Focus on Taxes...**" The income and taxes that you will defer will be making a lot more money while you are still young and working. With a traditional 401k, you will have more money to invest. In your younger years, it is logical that you will be putting a bigger portion of your savings into more aggressive investments such as mid-cap, small cap and emerging market funds which have a potential of yielding the biggest returns out of all asset classes of mutual funds during periods of economic expansions. Then as you grow older it follows suit that you should be allocating more of your savings towards more conservative investments.

Other factors such as changes in the tax rates and elimination of certain tax deductions are moot points. They are the big "unknown" at this point. The future of the U.S. income tax system and changes in the law are unknowable. Who knows whether or not charitable contributions, state and local taxes, mortgage interest and real estate tax deductions will still be in existence by the time you retire? I like taking what I can get right now than waiting for the future. I prefer not to convert my traditional 401k to a Roth because I want more money to invest right now. No one knows if the tax system will be favorable or not. The pendulum may swing the other way every 8 years or so. If your company offers both and you qualify for both, you may contribute 50/50 into a traditional and Roth 401k to diversify your lifetime tax expense on your retirement savings but only if your budget shows that you can afford to pay the taxes now.

Another huge factor you must consider when choosing between traditional and Roth retirement accounts is the state tax. With a Roth account, you pay the state taxes now. With a traditional account, you pay the taxes later, most likely when you retire. If you retire in a state that does NOT tax retirement income such as Florida, Nevada, Alaska, Texas, South Dakota, Washington and Wyoming (See Chapter, *OTHER RETIREMENT IDEAS* for more information) you forever escape, theoretically, paying the state tax on your retirement savings. I say "theoretically" because your state of residence when distribution is taken will prevail. With that said, there are some states that attempt to claw back taxes when a participant moves. Consult a tax attorney to find out the current tax law in your state. If your state does not claw back taxes, you've got it made. You've escaped the state tax on your traditional retirement account FOREVER! If you live in a high tax state such as New York, California, Connecticut, Illinois and New Jersey, then retire to Florida or Nevada, the state tax savings will be a big deal to most retirees.

Certain rules apply to Roth IRA and Roth 401k contributions. Your company's retirement plan administrator should be able to provide you with the necessary information on how to qualify for a Roth 401k and how to convert your traditional 401k into a Roth 401k. The IRS website below has current information but remember, rules particularly the income limits and contributions change almost every year so you will need to check the website for updates:
https://www.irs.gov/retirement-plans/roth-iras

With regard to your company's matching contributions to your 401k account, it does not matter how much your employer matches. Although on Chart 1, we project that your employer will contribute at least the safe harbor match which in 2016 is 100% of the first 3% of employee contribution and 50% of the next 2%, whatever it is, think of the company match as a bonus---free money. Maximizing contributions to your 401k plan whether your company matches zero or the maximum is an essential part of your financial wealth building game plan. Reducing expenses and increasing your income will help achieve your goal of contributing the maximum each year. The deferred tax benefit and the compounding interest you will earn is incredible.

According to Historical Market Data, the average annualized return of the S&P 500 Index was just about 10% for the past 42 years. With dividends reinvested, the returns are even more at 11.9%. The compound interest you will earn on your contributions over your working life cannot be matched by any other investment. If you can contribute close to the maximum, never touch the money and never lose any of the money you contributed, you don't have to bother with any other investment. You can simply sit back and watch your money grow till you retire.

If your employer does not offer a 401k account, you are at a disadvantage but you can still contribute the maximum into an IRA and Roth IRA Accounts. The maximum contribution at the time of writing is $5500 (plus $1000 catch up contribution, age 50 and older). Check in the IRS website about the qualifications and limitation of contributions.

https://www.irs.gov/retirement-plans/roth-comparison-chart

Earn at least 10% APY (annual percentage yield) on your savings

The S&P 500 average return for the past 42 years according to the following chart is just about 10%. The average annual return from inception (1926) through 2011 was 11.69%.

Chart 5

S & P 500 - 42 YEAR AVERAGE RETURNS (ACTUAL)

(SOURCE: http://www.1stock1.com/1stock1_141.htm)

Year	Ending Price	Gain or Loss	Percent Gain or Loss
1975	90.19	21.63	31.55%
1976	107.46	19.15	19.15%
1977	95.1	-12.36	-11.50%
1978	96.73	1.63	1.71%
1979	107.94	11.21	11.59%
1980	135.76	27.82	25.77%
1981	122.55	-13.21	-9.73%
1982	140.64	18.09	14.76%
1983	164.93	24.29	17.27%
1984	167.24	2.31	1.40%
1985	211.28	44.04	26.33%
1986	242.17	30.89	14.62%
1987	247.08	4.91	2.03%
1988	277.72	30.64	12.40%
1989	353.4	75.68	27.25%
1990	330.22	-23.18	-6.56%
1991	417.09	86.87	26.31%
1992	435.71	18.62	4.46%
1993	466.45	30.74	7.06%
1994	459.27	-7.18	-1.54%
1995	615.93	156.66	34.11%
1996	740.74	124.81	20.26%
1997	970.43	229.69	31.01%
1998	1229.23	258.8	26.67%
1999	1469.25	240.02	19.53%
2000	1320.28	-148.97	-10.14%
2001	1148.08	-172.2	-13.04%
2002	879.82	-268.26	-23.37%
2003	1111.92	232.1	26.38%
2004	1211.92	100	8.99%
2005	1248.29	36.37	3.00%
2006	1418.3	170.01	13.62%
2007	1468.36	50.06	3.53%
2008	903.25	-565.11	-38.49%
2009	1115.1	211.85	23.45%
2010	1257.64	142.54	12.78%
2011	1257.6	-0.04	0.00%
2012	1426.19	168.59	13.41%
2013	1848.36	422.17	29.60%
2014	2058.9	210.54	11.39%
2015	2043.94	-14.96	-0.73%
2016	2238.83	194.89	9.54%
			415.83%
AVERAGE			9.90%

For the 42-year period, with dividends reinvested, not adjusted for inflation, the annualized S&P 500 return is 11.9% (Source: https://dqydj.com/sp-500-return-calculator/).

Although the past is not a guarantee of future performance, there is a lot to be said about a 42-year history. You would have made 11.9% annualized returns if you just left your money alone in an S&P 500 Indexed Fund and never touched it for 42 years. Certain passively managed diversified, equity and growth funds made more than 12% APY. Check out the 40-year performances of funds in the Vanguard family of funds, Putnam, T. Rowe Price, MFS, Century, Pioneer, Fidelity and many others that returned more than 10% APY. Further examination of the preceding chart reveals that if you got out of the market during the years that the S&P 500 lost money and your savings earned zero interest instead of a negative yield, your average APY would have been 12.64% as per the following chart and approximately 15% with dividends reinvested:

Chart 6

S & P 500 - 42 YEAR AVERAGE RETURNS, WITHOUT THE NEGATIVE YEARS

(SOURCE: http://www.1stock1.com/1stock1_141.htm)

Year	Ending Price	Gain or Loss	Percent Gain or Loss
1975	90.19	21.63	31.55%
1976	107.46	19.15	19.15%
1977	95.1	-12.36	0.00%
1978	96.73	1.63	1.71%
1979	107.94	11.21	11.59%
1980	135.76	27.82	25.77%
1981	122.55	-13.21	0.00%
1982	140.64	18.09	14.76%
1983	164.93	24.29	17.27%
1984	167.24	2.31	1.40%
1985	211.28	44.04	26.33%
1986	242.17	30.89	14.62%
1987	247.08	4.91	2.03%
1988	277.72	30.64	12.40%
1989	353.4	75.68	27.25%
1990	330.22	-23.18	0.00%
1991	417.09	86.87	26.31%
1992	435.71	18.62	4.46%
1993	466.45	30.74	7.06%
1994	459.27	-7.18	0.00%
1995	615.93	156.66	34.11%
1996	740.74	124.81	20.26%
1997	970.43	229.69	31.01%
1998	1229.23	258.8	26.67%
1999	1469.25	240.02	19.53%
2000	1320.28	-148.97	0.00%
2001	1148.08	-172.2	0.00%
2002	879.82	-268.26	0.00%
2003	1111.92	232.1	26.38%
2004	1211.92	100	8.99%
2005	1248.29	36.37	3.00%
2006	1418.3	170.01	13.62%
2007	1468.36	50.06	3.53%
2008	903.25	-565.11	0.00%
2009	1115.1	211.85	23.45%
2010	1257.64	142.54	12.78%
2011	1257.6	-0.04	0.00%
2012	1426.19	168.59	13.41%
2013	1848.36	422.17	29.60%
2014	2058.9	210.54	11.39%
2015	2043.94	-14.96	0.00%
2016	2238.83	194.89	9.54%
			530.93%
AVERAGE			12.64%

If you follow my exit strategy in my book, ***THE SIMPLEST PATH TO WEALTH***

("Path2Wealth")

https://www.amazon.com/Simplest-Path-Wealth-Turn-Million-ebook/dp/B01KPQB0OS/ref=asap_bc?ie=UTF8

it is possible to earn 30% or more during the bull markets that follow recessions. There is a timetable in the book showing when to exit the market before the beginning of the bear market that follows a recession and when to get back into stocks close to the bottom of that bear market. For now, let's forget about 30% APY. Let's just say you only earned 10% APY instead of the negative yields the S&P 500 actually earned during those down years. Your average 42-year return would have been approximately 15.02% per annum as shown on the chart that follows (negative yields replaced with +10% gain) or approximately 18% with dividends reinvested.

Chart 7

S & P 500 - 42 YEAR AVERAGE RETURNS, 10% YIELD IN NEGATIVE YEARS

(SOURCE: http://www.1stock1.com/1stock1_141.htm)

Year	Ending Price	Gain or Loss	Percent Gain or Loss
1975	90.19	21.63	31.55%
1976	107.46	19.15	19.15%
1977	95.1	-12.36	10.00%
1978	96.73	1.63	1.71%
1979	107.94	11.21	11.59%
1980	135.76	27.82	25.77%
1981	122.55	-13.21	10.00%
1982	140.64	18.09	14.76%
1983	164.93	24.29	17.27%
1984	167.24	2.31	1.40%
1985	211.28	44.04	26.33%
1986	242.17	30.89	14.62%
1987	247.08	4.91	2.03%
1988	277.72	30.64	12.40%
1989	353.4	75.68	27.25%
1990	330.22	-23.18	10.00%
1991	417.09	86.87	26.31%
1992	435.71	18.62	4.46%
1993	466.45	30.74	7.06%
1994	459.27	-7.18	10.00%
1995	615.93	156.66	34.11%
1996	740.74	124.81	20.26%
1997	970.43	229.69	31.01%
1998	1229.23	258.8	26.67%
1999	1469.25	240.02	19.53%
2000	1320.28	-148.97	10.00%
2001	1148.08	-172.2	10.00%
2002	879.82	-268.26	10.00%
2003	1111.92	232.1	26.38%
2004	1211.92	100	8.99%
2005	1248.29	36.37	3.00%
2006	1418.3	170.01	13.62%
2007	1468.36	50.06	3.53%
2008	903.25	-565.11	10.00%
2009	1115.1	211.85	23.45%
2010	1257.64	142.54	12.78%
2011	1257.6	-0.04	10.00%
2012	1426.19	168.59	13.41%
2013	1848.36	422.17	29.60%
2014	2058.9	210.54	11.39%
2015	2043.94	-14.96	10.00%
2016	2238.83	194.89	9.54%
			630.93%
AVERAGE			15.02%

- Whether or not you follow the investment strategy in the book, ***"Path2Wealth"***, you should still be able to earn at least an average of 10% APY if you do not take your money out of mutual funds after they have lost 20% to 50% of their value during a negative year for stocks. If you wait 2 to 3 years, the value of your stocks should recover. If for some twist of fate you have to get to your money after your funds lost 50% value, it will take you several years to recover what you have lost since you will be selling devalued stocks. If you follow the timing system in the book, ***"Path2Wealth"***, you may avoid cyclical downturns and catastrophic losses of 30% or more when the economy goes into a recession. The timing strategy in the book is a way of recession proofing your retirement savings by developing a timeline for the next recession. While the economy is in a period of expansion, leave your money alone in stock mutual funds until an identifiable recession is in sight. Moving in and out of the stock market by trying to time dips and rebounds during an expansionary phase in our economy is a sure way to reduce your returns.

Asset allocation for a minimum 10% annual return

I prefer my portfolio to be self-directed so as to save the 2% to 3% a financial planner typically charges. The expertise these professionals provide is usually, 1) to determine your risk tolerance, 2) pick the appropriate stocks, bonds and mutual funds for your age, 3) periodically review your account for any life changes and objectives, 4) active management of your account by monitoring the funds' performance and management. I have had more luck investing my own money than when financial planners were directing my investments.

A 401k account usually has a limited number of funds in a plan but there are many more choices with an IRA at a bank or brokerage firm. If I have an IRA account I will invest my money in a group of highly rated mutual funds through E*Trade, Scottrade or TD Ameritrade following my own game plan as summarized in the next paragraph. At least with these discount brokers you do not have to pay the extra 2% to 3% fee. You will still pay the mutual fund fees which are interwoven within the funds themselves.

Summary:

- I try to maximize my contribution to my 401k account, which in 2016 is $18,000. I am dollar-cost-averaging into the stock market with my periodic contributions from every paycheck.
- I have my money in mutual funds not individual stocks. I have a moderately aggressive risk tolerance which means if I lost 50% of my money, I will not panic and withdraw the depreciated balance. I will ride the tide and wait it out until the stock market recovers which it inevitably does. I am more than 10 years away from retirement so I prefer to allocate my assets, 100% in stocks, 1/8 of my balance or 12.5% of the total into each of these categories of highly rated mutual funds: 1) Large-Cap Growth, 2) Large-Cap Value, 3) Mid-Cap Growth, 4) Mid-Cap Value, 5) Small-Cap Growth, 6) Small-Cap Value, 7) Balanced and 8) European Stock Fund. I selected each category from the

following family of funds: Vanguard, T. Rowe Price, Fidelity, Transamerica, John Hancock, Janus, Oppenheimer, Hartford, Invesco, Dreyfus, BlackRock, Janus, Franklin Templeton, Eaton Vance and American Century. The following website shows the best long-term performers in some of the most popular mutual fund categories:

http://money.usnews.com/funds.

Example of Allocation

$500,000 Portfolio, $62,500 in each of these funds:

Large Growth
Vanguard PRIMECAP Fund Adm (VPMAX)

Large Value
American Funds Mutual Fund R6 (RMFGX)

Mid-Cap Growth
Janus Enterprise N (JDMNX)

Mid-Cap Value
American Century NT MdCap Val Instl (ACLMX)

Small Cap Growth
Janus Triton Fund D (JANIX)

Small Cap Value
Vanguard Small-Cap Value Index FD (VISVX)

Balanced Fund
American Funds American Balanced Fund A (ABALX)

European Stock Fund
T. Rowe Price European Stock Fund (PRESX)

- I automatically rebalance my portfolio at the end of each quarter.

- I follow my exit strategy outlined in the book, "***Path2Wealth***"

Purchase Your Primary Residence

As a preface to this chapter, choose your principal residence with these five pointers in mind: 1) I will not buy this house as an investment, thinking that I will make a profit when I sell it. Those days of making a killing in real estate are gone. If it happens, lucky you. 2) I will buy a house that is nice and comfortable to live in and has no major defects such as radon, molds, sinking foundation, sink holes and pest infestation. 3) I will buy a house in a good neighborhood and that has a good school system and low taxes. 4) I will buy a house that is low maintenance so that I will not spend the entire weekend for its upkeep. 5) I will NOT buy a house next to crazy neighbors who can make my life miserable until I'm forced to move out. In other words, I will buy a house with "a forever house" in mind.

A house will likely be your single biggest investment ever. Statistically, buying a house is cheaper than renting. By the time you are ready to retire, the mortgage on the house will probably be paid off leaving you with a nice nest egg of a few hundred thousand dollars. This asset plus the millions in your retirement fund if you succeed in following the strategies in this book will provide you with a nice retirement income and a substantial estate you can leave your heirs. Buying your principal residence with a low interest mortgage loan is an investment that is hard to beat. The rent you would have paid would go instead towards servicing the loan. Towards interest which is tax deductible and towards the principal. As the principal is reduced, your equity increases. Your property may also go up in value by the time you are ready to sell. You will always be paying property tax but that is federal tax deductible also at the present time. The $250,000/$500,000 exclusion of gain from sale of a principal residence for singles/joint taxpayers is one of the best tax shelters that is still in existence as of publication of this book. Check on the IRS website for exceptions and changes to this U.S. tax code to make sure the law has not changed, (https://www.irs.gov/publications/p523/ar02.html)

Buying your principal residence that you can afford is different from other investments. This investment may go up or down in value but you still sleep in it. Think of your primary residence as your shelter, the roof over your head, your home, your sanctuary not an investment. The following generally accepted formula will give you an idea what price of a house you can afford by calculating your debt to income ratio:

Principal+Interest+Taxes+Insurance (PITI) $xxxx + all other monthly debt payments $xxxx = Total Monthly Debt Payments $xxxx , multiplied by 12 must not exceed 40% of your annual gross income (debt to income ratio). Example, your gross income is $100,000. PITI plus other monthly debt obligations must not exceed $40,000 a year or $3,333 a month. Many banks have been allowing over 40% debt to income ratio provided the applicant has an excellent credit record and pays a mortgage loan insurance which is usually 1% of the mortgage balance. This can be dangerous for the debtor. In the event of a financial reversal and loss of income and the home owner cannot continue making payments, the property may be foreclosed on by the mortgagee and sold as a distressed property. When this happens the home owner would most likely lose some or most of his equity in the property. In some states the mortgage holder may be able to go after the home owner for the deficiency in case the property is sold for less than the balance of the mortgage. Before buying a property it is important for the buyer to accurately assess job security and the prospect of increase or decrease in income in the future. Many homebuyers are confident enough about their job security and their future income that they buy houses they can hardly afford so that initially they become house poor, with a 50% debt to income ratio. This works out for some if their houses appreciate more than the average appreciation as they did in the eighties. On Chart 9, for our analysis we will be using 40% debt to income ratio.

CHART 9		Annualized	Monthly
Take home pay before 401k deduction		40,000	3,333
Rent or PITI & Other Recurring Monthly Debt Payments	40%	-16,000	-1,333
		Annualized	Monthly
Take home pay before 401k deduction		60,000	5,000
Rent or PITI & Other Recurring Monthly Debt Payments	40%	-24,000	-2,000
		Annualized	Monthly
Take home pay before 401k deduction		90,000	7,500
Rent or PITI & Other Recurring Monthly Debt Payments	40%	-36,000	-3,000

As shown on the preceding chart, if your gross pay is $90,000 a year, your combined monthly recurring debt payments should not be more than $3,000 a month. If you follow this percentage rule you should be safe and you should not be over-extended. A look-back accounting analysis of the finances of some of my friends and relatives reveals that most of them would have fared much better if they just followed the 40% maximum expense rule for monthly debt service. Many of them took on too much mortgage debt, some with debt to income ratio of 50% making them house poor, only to see the values of their houses plunge due to the real estate bubble burst. Do not purchase your primary residence if you will exceed 40% debt to income ratio. Take steps now to reduce your other expenses and still maintain a comfortable lifestyle. Refer to my book,

"DYNAMIC BUDGETING TECHNIQUES" ("DynBudgTech"). https://www.amazon.com/Dynamic-Budgeting-Techniques-expenses-double-ebook/dp/B01LZA9O3W/ref=sr_1_7?s=digital-text&ie=UTF8&qid=1499373868&sr=1-7&keywords=Arthur V. Prosper

The above-mentioned book has instructions on how to create a cash flow to find out where every dollar goes and a budget that should help you develop techniques that will help you reduce essential and non-essential expenses.

The way you can really compare owning to renting is by creating a Pros and Cons comparison table. Plug in real numbers to give you a better idea of where you will be after a period of time.

Pros and Cons of Owning

Pros: No landlord or landlady to deal with. You are at their mercy if you did something they don't like. If you make too much noise, scratch the walls, host too many parties they can increase your rent by 25% in one year or worse, kick you out when your lease is up. Moving from place to place is very stressful. A fixed rate mortgage loan is guaranteed for a period of time. You have more freedom to do what you want with your dwelling. You have bigger space and no stomping neighbors going up and down the stairs to deal with. It is great for do-it-yourselfers and for those who enjoy yard work and gardening. You will receive mortgage tax deduction, property tax deduction, have a sense of community; equity build up; appreciation; capital gains tax exemption when you sell; pride of ownership; availability of an equity loan for emergencies.

Cons: Loss of interest on the down payment and closing costs; depreciation; illiquid asset; it's stressful to buy and sell; broker's fee when you sell; maintenance costs; time you lose in maintenance; may be farther away from your place of work; higher insurance and utility costs; common fees; it's an albatross around your neck if you get divorced; you cannot instantly move out if a bad neighbor moves in; property taxes; you will lose your equity and your FICO scores will plunge if you can no longer afford the monthly payments and have to move out.

Doing the comparison in an excel spreadsheet and using realistic figures will give you a more accurate result. The following websites are very useful. You can enter your actual numbers to see the result but you must enter accurate variables.

http://www.nytimes.com/interactive/2014/upshot/buy-rent-calculator.html?_r=0

http://michaelbluejay.com/house/rentvsbuy.html

I entered my figures on the above websites, then I created the following excel table to verify my figures. The result is astonishing. I would lose $159,876.05 if I choose renting to owning on a 15-year projection. This does not even take into consideration the intangibles, some of which were enumerated under the subject "Pros and Cons".

Chart 8

15 Year Projection	OWNING	
4%, 15 Year Fixed		
Price of Dwelling	350,000	
Down Payment	70,000	
Net Loan	280,000	
Annual Percentage Rate (APR)	4%	
Monthly Payment (Principal & Interest)	2,071	
Total Payments	372,803	1
Interest Expense after 15 years = $92,803.40		
Less Income Tax benefit on Interest @ 15%	-13,921	2
Real Estate Taxes, Avg $8400/year	126,000	3
Less Income Tax benefit on R/E Taxes @ 15%	-18,900	4
Maintenance & Repairs, Avg. $3500/year	52,500	5
Homeowner's Insurance, Avg. $1500/year	22,500	6
(a) Total Monthly Expenditure, 15 years (Add 1 to 6)	**540,983**	
Down Payment	70,000	
Closing Costs, 3%	10,500	
Renting a Comparable Dwelling		
15 Year Projection	**RENTING**	
Initial Rent at $1900/mo., 3% Annual Increases	424,055	
Renter's Insurance, Avg $800/year	12,000	
(b) Total Monthly Expenditure after 15 years	**436,055**	
Difference in Total Expenditure (A-B)	104,928	
Renter's Monthly Savings ($104,928/180 mos.)	583	
Monthly Savings + Interest @ 8% APR	198,067	7
Less: Capital Gains Tax 15%	-29,710	8
Downpayment & Closing costs + Interest @ 8% APR	255,360	9
Less: Capital Gains Tax 15%	-38,304	10
Renter's Cash on hand after 15 years (Add 7 to 10)	385,413	11
Property value after 15 years at an		
average 3% per year increase..	545,289	
(Single Individual Capital Gains Exemption on profit=$250,000)		
Owner's Cash on hand after 15 years	545,289	12
Owner's Advantage vs. Renter after 15 years (#12 less # 11)	**$159,876**	

Chart 8 only shows a 15-year projection. After 15 years, I practically live rent free. I will still pay real estate taxes which at the time of writing are still tax deductible and I will continue to pay for repair and maintenance and higher insurance and utilities than a renter. But my home "may" continue to appreciate too as years go by.

Brian Lund, freelance writer wrote this article on July 19, 2014, "The Worst Investment You Can Make: Buying a Home". https://www.aol.com/article/finance/2014/07/19/the-worst-investment-you-can-make-buying-a-home/20932947/

Or google search: "BRIAN LUND THE WORST INVESTMENT YOU CAN MAKE"

In his article, Lund claims that you will end up saving $3 million if you rented a comparable house instead of owning one for $350,000. That is, if you invested the savings you will realize by renting instead of owning a comparable house. Lund adds, ***"Of course there are numerous tweaks you can make to this scenario -- for example, factoring in your home's price appreciation or the tax benefits -- but no matter how you slice it, owning a home doesn't come anywhere close to making financial sense."***

I can cite a few problems with his article:

1. He uses a 30 year fixed rate at 4.5% interest. At the time of writing, you can get a much lower rate for a 15 year fixed.
2. He assumes that the rent for a comparable dwelling is 75% of the monthly principal and interest payment and has no provision for rent increases over a period of 30 years which is unrealistic.
3. He does not factor in the loss of interest mortgage deduction and real estate tax deduction that will generally put the homeowner into a lower tax bracket. Conversely, he does not consider the fact that a renter will pay tax on the interest his savings earns.
4. He assumes zero appreciation for your home. There is no way to predict if housing is going up or down but assuming zero appreciation over 30 years is not reasonable. According to the National Association of Realtors (NAR) existing homes appreciated 5.4% annually from 1968 to

2009 on the average. The nationwide average annual increase of existing homes from 1987 to 2009 according to the Case-Schiller Index was 3.4%. Also, at the time of writing, there is a $250,000 ($500,000 couple) capital gains exclusion on the profit realized on the sale of a principal residence. See IRS Publication 523, https://www.irs.gov/taxtopics/tc701.html
Check on the above mentioned IRS website to see if you qualify for the exclusion. On the other hand, interest on savings is taxed as ordinary income.

5. He neglects to consider that after 15 years when your house is paid off, you pretty much live rent free. Yes, you will still pay for real estate taxes, upkeep and higher insurance and utilities than a renter pays but the house is yours. Real estate taxes will continue to reduce your taxable income even after mortgage payments end if you itemize.
6. Finally, he fails to consider that many people will not save the savings they will realize by being a renter. They will find a way to spend it.

In his article "Five Things You NEED to Know before Buying a House", James Altucher declares, ***"I hate buying houses. I don't "hate" many things. But I've lost millions of dollars buying houses. The stress is unbearable when you need to sell. And you have no money when you need it. It's a prison. The white picket fence is the prison bars. The bank is the guards looking in. And the need to protect your family keeps you in a solitary confinement of guilt and anxiety and stress."***

Who can lose millions of dollars in real estate? The truth is James is really telling the truth. He really had a string of bad luck that most people will never experience. No one can lose millions of dollars in real estate without really trying. Especially not if the subject real estate is your principal residence. James Altucher indeed lost at least $2 million in real estate. He was unlucky enough to buy at the wrong place at the wrong time. He was a victim of a "perfect storm". Real Estate burnt him that is why he hates real estate and won't go near it anymore. As the story goes, Mr. Altucher bought a $1.8 million condo in the Tribeca section of Manhattan which is in the downtown area not far from

Chinatown. Then he put in at least $1 million in renovations. Shortly thereafter, the 9/11 attacks happened. He ended up selling his condo for $1 million. So I guess he was not exaggerating after all. Contrast his luck with that of a distant relative of mine who is in the advertising industry and claims NOT to know anything about real estate. True story except, we will call her Jane. She bought a pre-construction 2-bedroom condo at the Orion building near the Port Authority bus terminal in NYC. Jane went into contract in 2006 for a pre-construction sale price of $900,000. When the unit was ready for occupancy in late 2007, its value had already increased to $1.2 million. The building had a long waiting list of buyers. For some reason not disclosed to me, 3 years later, Jane went into contract to buy another 2 bedroom unit at the just completed Rushmore building on Riverside Blvd in the upper West Side. The pre-construction price of her unit was $1 million. To make a long story short, she sold her Orion unit for $1.7 million and bought the Rushmore unit for $1 million. How is that for buying low and selling high to make a hefty profit? And here's the kicker. She got a 3% 15-year fixed mortgage loan and her 2 bedroom condo is now worth at least $2 million. Call it fortuitous timing or the luck of the Irish, but certainly, NYC real estate treated Jane much better than it did James.

I admit I've lost thousands (not millions) of dollars in rental properties which is why I will NOT go near them, but rarely can you go wrong in buying your own house. Do the math and make sure to consider all the different factors and you will see that typically, owning your home is cheaper than renting a similar dwelling. With regard to Altucher's calling a house a prison, an apartment is also a prison only smaller. The landlord is the warden looking in. You can be thrown out of jail within months if you do something the warden does not like. On the other hand, maybe you can stay for 3 years in your house even if you stop paying the mortgage. It takes a long time for banks to go through the foreclosure and eviction process. There are many delaying tactics you can employ to delay foreclosure and eviction. Even after foreclosure the bank may have a hard time throwing you out on the street.

Location, location, location

The adage, location, location, location is true, true, true. Two exactly similar homes built on the same date will appreciate differently depending on their location. This is the number one rule in real estate. Location is the greatest determining factor in the value of a property. You can fix up a house but you cannot fix up its location.

Look for a house in a nice neighborhood with good schools and a low crime rate and close to your place of work. Check out the following factors: the school district's rating, the crime rate, distance to your place of work, distance to low income housing, commercial and industrial properties, farms, factories, schools, cemetery, railroad tracks, freeways, subway stations, landfills, garbage dumps, recycling, bars, restaurants, main thoroughfares and sports arenas. Determine if the neighborhood is economically stable and observe if the neighborhood is composed of similar types of properties. A house in a fairly homogeneous neighborhood will retain its value better than a similar home in a neighborhood where there are apartments, condominiums and businesses. Check out if the residents take pride in ownership by maintaining their lawns, roofs and exterior of their houses. If the homes have poor landscaping and discarded mattresses, junk car parts and old appliances litter some of the yards, I would not move there. Buy the worst house on the best block. If you live in the Snowbelt choose a house whose driveway faces south east to help the sun melt the ice and snow. If your driveway faces north, you will need a lot of ice-melt, rock salt and de-icer. Houses with south east exposure are better in that part of the country. Make sure you can live with your neighbors. It will be hard to move out after you've moved in. Drive around the neighborhood all hours of the day and night, on weekdays as well as on weekends to observe if there are undesirable individuals hanging out on street corners. Go to the local police precinct and to the city or municipal building. Ask the police and town clerk questions about the specific street where the house you are considering is located. In most cases, they should be glad to provide information from their own personal knowledge of that neighborhood. The county where the house is located may compile a crime report for different neighborhoods which may be available online.

I prefer a house in the middle of the tract or at the end of a cul-de-sac to one located on the corner. Corners have more traffic and less privacy. Compare property taxes. Real estate taxes can vary a lot. This is an expense you will be paying for a very long time and when the time comes to sell your house the buyer will be looking at the tax expense as well. It would be necessary to put a real dollar figure as well as imaginary dollar value on the pros and cons to determine the amount of money you will really save over a period of time. If you move closer to your place of work, how much money will you save in fuel? How much time will you save in your daily commute? How do they translate in real dollars? You won't be hearing neighbors going up and down the stairs if you own your own house. How much in imaginary dollars is that worth to you?

If you already own a house and plan to stay in your house for at least 7 years, refinance your mortgage if you can get a rate that is at least 2% lower than what you have now and there are no closing costs. Each time you refinance, you will be resetting the mortgage clock to day one. So you will extend the period of your loan unless you are refinancing from a 30 year mortgage to a 20 or 15 year loan. Any extra cash you may receive out of refinancing your home must be used, 1) to pay off credit card debt or other high interest debts, 2) for repair and maintenance of your home, 3) to fund your retirement account. It is better if you do not take on extra debt. Add the monthly savings you may realize, if any, from refinancing your home to your contribution to your retirement account. Keep filling up your pot of gold as much as you can.

As part of my financial master plan, as your income increases and you constantly end up with a monthly surplus even after maximizing your 401k contributions, consider moving up to a better house in a better neighborhood with a better school system. See the chapter,

"Planning for College" in the book, ***"Living Rich and Loving It"***

https://www.amazon.com/Living-Rich-Loving-healthy-balanced-ebook/dp/B01GORIB4Y/ref=sr_1_6?s=digital-text&ie=UTF8&qid=1507563906&sr=1-6&keywords=Arthur V. Prosper

This chapter discusses the importance of a good school system in preparation for college education for your children. It would be better to put that monthly surplus into your own home than wasting it on a Benz or Bimmer, or giving away a big portion of it to the taxman.

Collect Social Security benefits at the right time

The Bipartisan Budget Act of 2015 included two major changes to Social Security benefits for those who were born after January 1, 1954. Because of the changes, the correct timing for collecting social security benefits became simpler. In general, you should wait as long as possible to collect social security to take advantage of the 8% additional benefit increase each year you delay collecting after FRA (full retirement age). If you wait till 70, you will collect the maximum benefits which will be an additional 32% of what you would have received at FRA. If you cannot wait till 70 to get your maximum benefit, at least wait until you reach FRA. The following table shows the FRA for your age:

- If you were born in 1937 or earlier, Full Retirement Age is 65.
- 1938: 65 and 2 months
- 1939: 65 and 4 months
- 1940: 65 and 6 months
- 1941: 65 and 8 months
- 1942: 65 and 10 months
- 1943--1954: 66
- 1955: 66 and 2 months
- 1956: 66 and 4 months
- 1957: 66 and 6 months
- 1958: 66 and 8 months
- 1959: 66 and 10 months
- If you were born in 1960 or later, Full Retirement Age is 67.

At present, you may begin collecting SS benefits at 62 but your benefits will be reduced by 1 to 25% of the benefits you would have received at FRA. The percent of reduction will depend on the number of months you are shy of your FRA. The SSA website, https://www.ssa.gov/ has a lot of resources that can help you calculate your benefits, estimate the best age to start receiving retirement benefits and other things to consider to help you make a decision. The rules have not changed for individuals born before January 2, 1954. Since the various SS benefit claiming strategies are complex especially for couples, widows and widowers and divorced people, I created the following table to show my own personal claiming preference for people born on or after January 2, 1954:

Chart 10

SOCIAL SECURITY ROAD MAP	CLAIMING STRATEGY
SINGLE NEVER MARRIED	Wait at least until full retirement age.
MARRIED	Wait at least until full retirement age, for the following reasons: "File and suspend" strategy was eliminated as of May 1, 2016. A married person who reaches FRA must actually collect benefits in order for the spouse to collect spousal benefits. "Restricted applications" strategy which allows a spouse to file an application to claim spousal benefit but defer collecting their own until age 70, was also eliminated. If you were born before January 2, 1954, check with the SSA for the exceptions and what options may be available to you. https://www.ssa.gov/
MARRIED AT LEAST 10 YEARS, DIVORCED AT LEAST 2 AND CURRENTLY SINGLE	Wait at least until FRA. Then file for either your own benefits or for spousal benefits. SSA will pay the higher of the two.

DIVORCED, HAS REMARRIED & CURRENTLY MARRIED	Wait at least until FRA. You cannot claim under your ex-spouse's benefits since you are currently married.
WIDOW/WIDOWER	Wait till FRA if you can. You may receive reduced survivor's benefits as early as age 60. If you are disabled, benefits can begin as early as age 50. If you wait till FRA, you will collect the same amount your deceased spouse was collecting at the time of death. If your spouse did not start collecting benefits yet at the time of death, you will receive the higher of 100% of your spouse's maximum benefits at FRA or 100% of your own. If you start collecting prior to FRA your benefits will be further reduced if you earn more than $16,920 a year. Click on the link below for more detailed information:

https://www.ssa.gov/planners/survivors/ifyou5.html

SURVIVING DIVORCED SPOUSE, MARRIED AT LEAST 10 YEARS, CURRENTLY SINGLE OR REMARRIED AFTER THE AGE OF 60	You can get benefits just the same as a widow or widower, but check on the website above for updates on qualifications and various options. Rules and limits often change.

The SSA states "...the rules are complicated and laws change..." They advise that individuals should call their number, 1-800-772-1213 for up to date information before making any decisions.

There are many different ways to collect your benefits and there are many factors that can influence your decision and timing as to when you should apply for benefits. There are personal considerations that are unique to your situation such as your health, financial needs, income and tax rate. The SSA cannot give you advice. They can only provide the facts. Once the facts are known pertaining to your own unique situation, you can compare your options by putting the numbers on a spreadsheet.

There is no doubt that pressure is on Congress to keep looking at ways to keep the social security system solvent for the foreseeable future. The ideas that were thrown around during the 2016 Presidential Primaries included increasing retirement age and increasing the wage limit, which in 2016 was $118,500. The legislators closed what they considered loopholes in the system, i.e. "file and suspend" and "restricted applications".

File-and-Suspend

The "file-and-suspend" strategy worked best for married couples that had a significant difference in their social security earnings records. Under the law in effect until May 1, 2016:

1. A higher-earning spouse claims social security benefits based on his or her earnings record. Once that claim is made, the lower-earning spouse applies for a spousal benefit based on the higher-earning spouse's earnings record.
2. The higher-earning spouse files for benefits then voluntarily chooses to suspend until age 70 to maximize his or her own benefits. The lower-earning spouse continues to receive the higher spousal benefit during the suspension period, and the higher-earning spouse accumulates more retirement credits equivalent to an 8% annual increase.
3. When the higher-earning spouse dies, the lower-earning spouse is eligible for survivor's benefits based on the deceased spouses' increased benefit.
4. The higher-earning spouse may suspend the benefit until age 70. At that time, or anytime between the initial application and age 70 the suspended benefits are claimed retroactively. The receipt of the suspended benefits are only delayed not lost. As of

May 1, 2016, the higher earning spouse can no longer file and suspend. He or she must actually file and collect to allow the lower earning spouse to collect spousal benefits. There is no longer an advantage for the higher earner to defer benefits to age 70.

Restricted Application

The "restricted application" strategy worked best for married couples that have similar social security earnings records and are about the same age.
Using this strategy allows the lower-earning spouse, at full retirement age, to claim a spousal benefit based on the other spouse's earnings record. At the same time, the lower-earning spouse will postpone receiving their own benefit based upon their earnings record. As with the "file-and-suspend" strategy, the lower-earning spouse's delayed benefits will increase by approximately 8% a year until turning age 70 or before if that couple decides it is no longer an advantage to defer the benefits to age 70.

If you were born before January 2, 1954, check with the SSA how the new rules affect you. Click on the website below to find out the approximate value of your social security benefits: https://www.forbes.com/sites/baldwin/2016/03/15/whats-your-social-security-benefit-worth/#7a24d6c464d8

PART II – How to save at least $1000 a month

Get Rid of All Your Consumer Debts

As long as you have non-mortgage debts, you will continue to struggle in finding the doorway to financial independence. You should not be paying monthly installments on your credit card debts and other consumer debts such as pay day loans, car loans, department store loans, furniture and home improvement loans. Pay them in full right now from other sources or ask your creditors for a reduction or complete forgiveness of your debts. Refer to my book, "**STOP PAYING YOUR CREDIT CARDS**" for more information on debt reduction/forgiveness negotiation.

https://www.amazon.com/dp/B019ZY3D1E/ref=rdr_kindle_ext_tmb

Do not charge anything on your credit cards if you cannot afford to pay the balance in full when you receive your statement. It is not OK to borrow money from revolving credit accounts and pay only the minimum monthly installment. As long as you keep a balance on your credit card accounts, it will be hard to achieve your financial goals because you are throwing away hard earned cash. Some people think: "If I can afford to pay the monthly minimum payment, I can afford to borrow (even at 25% APR)". NO, it's NOT! If you are constantly borrowing and charging purchases on your credit cards and paying only the minimum each month, chances are your credit card balances will continue to increase and you will never achieve financial independence. Paying 25% APR interest on your credit card debt is a waste of money. Getting rid of your credit card debts is your first step on the road to a successful retirement. If you cannot afford to pay your credit card debt in full when the statement comes, you cannot afford the purchase. Stop using your credit card. Borrow money from your 401k account or obtain money by refinancing your house if you can to pay off the high interest credit card balances. A debt-free lifestyle is an integral part of the financial game plan. If you simply have no available cash to pay off your balances and have no source of funds, plan B is to sell any hard assets you may have such as a car, furniture, jewelries, anything of value and drastically reduce your expenses. Selling anything valuable to you is a hard choice and a big sacrifice but it has to be made to get you back on track to your destination which is financial independence. Plan C is to increase your income. My book, **"DynBudgTech"** has specific strategies on how to reduce discretionary expenses and how to make extra money in your spare time. Plan D is to stop paying your credits cards and beg the creditors for a reduction or forgiveness of your debt. This is the last resort. This move will negatively affect your credit and your FICO scores will tumble. This can set you back several years and may prevent you from obtaining a home mortgage loan. Click on the link below to get more information on how I mollified the effect of the negative information on my credit report. See the Chapter,

"**How to Mitigate Negative Credit Report**" in the book **Debt Forgiveness Volume 2**: https://www.amazon.com.au/DEBT-FORGIVENESS-Chapter-CREDITORS-DECIDE-ebook/dp/B01ACTBTIU

Reduce Your Taxes

Throughout my life, I make it a habit to learn every possible legal tax deduction, tax credit and tax loophole there is in the tax codes to make sure I am not overpaying my taxes. I do not want to pay a penny more than I have to. Much to my surprise, many people especially younger taxpayers have no idea what expenses can be deducted from earnings. A twenty something tax payer recently asked me, "Can I deduct my rent from my wages?" A fifty five year old lady told me, "I read somewhere I can deduct for my mother who lives with me..." "How long has she lived with you and do you contribute more than 50% of her support?" I asked. She replied, "She has been living with me continuously for 15 years and I pay at least 75% of her support". So it turns out that she could have been claiming her mother as a dependent for 15 years but the topic never came up at tax filing time because the tax preparer never asked and she did not know to ask. She only became curious and asked me the question when she came across the article in some magazine in the waiting room of her gynecologist's office. Many tax preparers do not ask their clients the questions they are supposed to ask. They bang out as many returns as they can get out during the tax season, collect their fee and have a nonchalant attitude about how much tax their clients are paying and how much money they can potentially save them. Hey, it's not their money. Even worse the attitude of many younger workers is not to ask the tax preparer any questions because, "He knows his job". I recently encountered a young couple at a party who casually discussed their tax situation with me. I overheard the discussion when the wife who works as a nurse said, "I'm busting my chops working so many overtime hours and the government is taking so much of it, maybe it is better if I did not work overtime at all". When I joined the conversation and got into their details I found out they have a combined family income of $145,000, two dependent children, and a $285,000 mortgage on their property and they paid over $20,000 in federal tax. I immediately said to myself that there must be something wrong somewhere. So I offered to review their tax return for free. It turned out that the tax preparer took the standard exemption of $16,200 and the standard deduction of $12,600. That's it. Their tax bill would have been cut in half had they taken the itemized deductions. I asked them why the tax preparer did not itemize and deduct the mortgage interest, state tax, charitable contributions, unreimbursed employee expenses, after school child care expense, etc., etc., etc. The husband replied, "Well, he did not ask any questions and we did not think of asking him any questions. After all he is a CPA and he knows what he's doing. We were afraid he might get insulted if we asked...besides he had a long waiting list of clients and he just accommodated us". "Oh what a waste of $10,000!" I said to myself. I offered to file an amended return for them so they may recover the $10,000 over-payment, but the husband said his wife is afraid because they might get audited. "She considers it water under the bridge", he added. Sadly, next year they will again over pay their taxes. They have a misconception that they should not be paying less as a percentage of their gross income, than what they used to pay as single taxpayers. Although they now have many legitimate deductions as a married couple with two children and a mortgage on their house, they are refusing to take the deductions for fear that they are doing something wrong---they think they would be cheating the government and that they will get caught by the IRS.

Because of this experience I compiled the following short check-list. If you think any of the tax credits apply to you or you may have incurred any of the deductible expenses on the list, discuss them with your tax preparer:

Check list:

- Maximize your deferred retirement contributions
- Ask your employer if an H.S.A. (Health Savings Account) is available through your company. If not, ask him how one may be set up. This is one of the most beneficial and less known tax favored accounts that you can set up to defer taxable income. Learn more in Chapter, "**Enroll in a H.S.A. (Health Savings Accounts**"
- Make sure that you have the correct dependents
- Business losses
- Real Estate Investment losses
- Capital Loss Carryover
- Gambling losses not to exceed your gambling gains

- Excess SS and Medicare taxes (often if you have 2 or more jobs)
- Student loan interest payments
- K-12 classroom and professional development expenses
- Job-related moving expenses
- Alimony payments
- Early withdrawal penalty (Box 2 Form 1099-INT or 1099-OID)
- IRA, SEP-IRA, Simple IRA, and Keogh contributions
- Health insurance premiums if you are self employed
- Attorney's fees related to certain discrimination claims
- Attorney's fees related to certain whistleblower awards from the IRS
- Home mortgage interest (1098 or statement)
- State and local income taxes
- Real estate and personal property taxes
- Sales taxes
- Unreimbursed job-related expenses including subscriptions, organization dues, uniform, home office, utilities & office supplies
- Job-search expenses
- Charitable donations, cash, clothing, books, appliances, furniture, etc.
- Expenses incurred as a volunteer for a charitable organization
- Medical and dental expenses
- Health insurance premiums if not deducted from your gross salary
- Casualty or theft loss
- Depreciation expense on an asset used in an investment activity

- State and local sales taxes in excess of state and local income taxes
- Mortgage insurance premiums
- Points paid on purchase of principal residence
- Real estate taxes paid
- Tax preparation expenses
- Safe deposit fees
- Legal expenses
- Investment expenses
- Hobby expenses
- Fees, subscriptions, tools connected with any income producing activity
- Credit/debit card tax payment convenience fee
- Estate tax paid on income in respect of a decedent
- Unrecovered pension investment
- Bond premiums
- Losses on certain debt instruments
- Child and dependent care expenses
- Retirement savings contribution credit (saver's credit)
- Adoption expenses
- Energy efficient home improvements
- Tuition for college or higher education (Form 1098-T)
- Child and dependent care credit
- Plug-in electric drive motor vehicle credit
- Foreign taxes paid
- Health insurance for displaced worker
- First-time home buyer credit in Washington, DC
- Low income housing credit (Form 8609 & 8586)

This check list was compiled at the time of writing. Some of the items on this list may have been revised, amended or discontinued. Check with your tax preparer and in the IRS website for updates. If you think you have any of the aforementioned deductions, make a list of the amounts and do not hesitate to give it to your tax preparer during your initial meeting. A good tax professional will not be offended that you are pointing out what may turn out as valid deductions and tax credits that he may not know about. In summary, to minimize your tax bill, 1) maximize your contribution to your tax deferred retirement plan, 2) if you constantly receive big refunds after tax filing, reduce the amount of your "federal tax withheld" by increasing your exemptions so that you are not overpaying your taxes throughout the year, 3) take advantage of all legal tax deductions, tax shelters, tax credits and loopholes.

****UPDATE**** ***The passage of the tax reform bill now officially known as The Tax Cuts and Jobs Act of 2017, Public Law No. 115-97, in which the tax brackets were changed reducing the tax burden of most individual taxpayer only proves that tax consideration should never lord it over a sound retirement strategy. Future tax burden is unknowable. You should not plan your investment and retirement strategy based on the current enacted tax law. The pendulum swings the other way about every eight years depending on which party is in power. These lower tax rates will expire in 2025 unless renewed by the incoming 2026 officials of the legislative and executive branches. It may or may not happen. The retirement strategy in this book will prove to be sound no matter what the tax system is. For more information, also see Chapter,*** **"How does the new tax law affect the retirement strategies in this book?"**

Reduce life, disability, health, auto and homeowner's insurance

Term life insurance is the best and the most cost effective way to protect your family when you die. Whole life insurance is very expensive and will take a bigger bite off of your budget over the years. Contrary to the rule of thumb that death benefits to your beneficiaries should equal 10 to 12 times annual household income, my advice is to buy only 7 times annual household income. You will save a lot of money in premiums. There is a big difference in the cost of a 12 x income policy vs. a 7 x income. This concept is explained in my book, **"DynBudgTech",** under Chapter, "**Term Life Insurance**". Ideas and strategies for reducing the cost of disability, medical, dental auto and home insurance are also discussed in the book. If you shop around and get the right blend of coverage for your auto and property insurance you can literally cut your premiums in half.

Enroll in a H.S.A. (Health Savings Accounts)

HSA is a tax favored account which you can set up in conjunction with a compatible health insurance plan. If your company does not have an HSA compatible health insurance plan, ask your HR department if they can set this up for your organization. Your company's group insurance policy may add this option to your insurance choices without extra cost in premiums. An HSA is one of the best tax shelters still in existence today. At the time of writing, if you qualify, you may be able to shelter up to $4,350 ($7,750 family plan) of taxable income through this tax exempt trust. The limits increase every year. Check with your HR department and on the IRS website below to make sure the law has not changed:

https://www.irs.gov/publications/p969/ar02.html

These are the eligibility requirements:

- Must be covered by an HSA-compatible health plan
- Not covered by other health insurance
- Not enrolled in Medicare
- Is not claimed as a dependent on someone else's tax return
    - Children cannot establish an HSA
    - Eligible spouses can establish their own HSA

To qualify as an HSA compatible policy a health insurance plan must be a high deductible health plan (HDHP). As an example, a plan that has an annual deductible of $2,500 single and $5,000 family will qualify as an HDHP. This means that you will have to pay for any medical expenses including doctor's visits co-pay, emergency room visits and prescription drug costs out of your HSA account until you reach the annual deductible. There are preventive care benefits that are not subject to the annual deductible. Please check the IRS website for more information.

Here are the benefits of an HSA account:

- There are no income restrictions.
- HSA funds are not forfeited, they roll over year to year.
- Tax is deferred on contributions and earnings.
- Distributions used for qualified medical expenses are tax free.
- The funds are portable. They go with you if you leave your present employer.

- After the age of 65, you can use the funds for any purpose without penalty but those distributions will be subject to income tax.

Check the IRS website for penalties for unauthorized use of funds and tax treatment of excess contributions. This tax favored account has a potential of adding a lot more money into your pot of gold otherwise known as your retirement savings.

Reduce your children's college costs

College cost is one of the biggest expenses a family will have. It will bite off a big chunk of your income and savings if you do not take the appropriate steps. Here are a few things you can do:

1. First, realize that college is not for everyone. If you think your child's talents and gifts from God are not geared toward pursuing a 4 year college degree, i.e. they are not college material, there are many other alternatives such as starting a business, going to trade or vocational school, being an artist, getting an associate degree, law enforcement, taking online courses, going to work, joining the military or AmeriCorps. Your children will do just as well and succeed even without a college degree as long as they find something that they can be passionate about. After all, Morley Safer, Richard Branson, Henry Ford, Walt Disney, Rush Limbaugh, Bill Gates and Steve Jobs did not graduate from college. Here are just a few jobs that can generate a lot of income which do not require a 4 year college degree: Electrician, welder, landscaper, nurse's aide, phlebotomist, dental hygienist, personal trainer, model, martial arts instructor, tour guide, carpenter, plumber, painter, Court interpreter, auto mechanic, aircraft maintenance assistant, air traffic controller, flight attendant, inventor, real estate broker, MRI technologist, roofer, truck driver, care giver, casino dealer, butcher, bass fisherman, mail carrier, journeyman, funeral director, barber or hairdresser, manicurist and pedicurist, skin care specialist, computer repair technician, IT Technician, graphic designer, stage manager, private investigator, home inspector, and many more...too many to mention.
2. If your children are college material, take the following steps as soon as possible:
    a. If your children are not in high school yet, consider moving into a highly rated public high school district in your state. Not only will you get more scholarship offers but it will better prepare your child for college. College is different than high school and many students drop out before the freshman year is over.

b. Get your children interested in extracurricular activities in school, in sports, academic clubs, debate teams, student body, band, music and drama.
c. Get your children interested in volunteer work and community service. If you contact your church, temple, synagogue, hospitals and local government you can specify a specific time your child will be available each week and the administrators will work with you. Even if your children accomplish this only in their senior year, it can still make a difference on their resume.
d. Let your children accept summer jobs as camp counsellor, waiter, dish washer, cook, care giver, office clerk, carpenter, landscaper, driver, etc., etc. This will show the college that your child has some degree of responsibility. This will look good on their applications.
e. Improve your children's SAT or ACT scores. Most colleges and universities publish the average SAT and ACT scores of their incoming freshmen. The following website shows the averages of hundreds of colleges and universities: https://www.powerscore.com/sat/help/average_test_scores.cfm

   Your children can take several steps to improve their scores. There are many books and study guides and practice courses designed to improve SAT and ACT scores. There are practice tests you can buy just by surfing the internet. The Official SAT Study Guide DVD edition or The Official SAT Study Guide 2nd edition are good examples. They can also take the Princeton Review, Kaplan or other college prep study courses. The following are useful websites which should all help the student develop test-taking skills:
   http://www.erikthered.com/tutor/practice.html
   https://www.graphite.org/website/number2com
   https://www.khanacademy.org/test-prep/sat

   If you can afford it, it is worth paying whatever these books and courses will cost you. In the long run, the benefit your children will gain from getting higher scores will more than pay for the costs.

f. Check with the high school guidance counsellors which colleges accept graduates from their high school. Some colleges and universities sometimes seek out students from a particular high school. Talk to parents of previous graduates of the high school about their college search experiences to see if they would recommend the college their children eventually ended up in. You will get a lot of useful information that can potentially save you thousands of dollars. You will also get an earful from parents who are not satisfied with the colleges their children are attending. You have to choose carefully because colleges are like dictatorships. For example, if you raised your children in a conservative household, they may constantly butt heads with college professors who have liberal views. They will either get bad grades, drop out or finish college a different person than the person you enrolled. They can be brainwashed from being conservative into being a progressive...and vice versa. This is an important factor in choosing a college. Google: "Most liberal and conservative colleges".
g. Many other factors will influence your college choice besides tuition and board such as: incidental expenses and transportation when considering schools that are out of your state, additional tuition fees for out of state students, student population, ethnic and racial composition, male to female ratio and the school's reputation for the degree your children will pursue, financial aid package. The US News and World Report website below provides additional information:
http://www.usnews.com/education

h. Be more analytical when it comes to evaluating your choices. After compiling a list of schools that have a good reputation for the degrees your children want to pursue, create a comparison spreadsheet with the following columns: Name of

College, Rank, No. of Students, + Tuition Fees, - Financial Aid Package, = Net After Financial Aid, + Estimated Travel and Additional Costs, = Net Annual Tuition & Travel and Miscellaneous Expenses. An example of this evaluation analysis is shown in the following book:

"LIVING RICH AND LOVING IT" ("LiveRich"), https://www.amazon.com/Living-Rich-Loving-healthy-balanced-ebook/dp/B01GORIB4Y/ref=asap_bc?ie=UTF8
There are many other ideas on how to minimize college costs in the above-mentioned book.

Avoid Conspicuous Consumption

Since I want to retire rich, I avoid buying products that have these labels associated with them: status symbol, brand name, upscale, designer, exclusive, limited edition, signature collection, luxury, prime, high society, etc. etc. etc. First, I am not willing to pay a premium for products for their "Veblen Good" value. These are goods that cost more than other products because of their snob appeal. They are bought by status-conscious consumers. Second, I do not think I gain the respect of others by using Veblen Goods. Third, I know the difference between "necessity and luxury". Finally, I know what to do with my budget surplus, and that is to put it into my pot of gold, i.e. my retirement account instead of throwing it into a luxury car. Why should I buy a Mercedes Benz S-Class for $100,000 when a $35,000 Consumer Reports highly rated Chevy Impala would do? A snobbish reader will probably scoff at this statement but no amount of interior comfort and luxury or amazing handling, performance and technology can convince me to shell out an extra $65,000 for a car. I am street smart and living rich in my books does not have to include driving a $100,000 luxury car. Perhaps a luxury car to some people represents power and success, not to me. And I don't have to keep up with the Joneses. Perhaps a luxury car makes up for deficiencies some people have. I will be quite content with a Chevy Impala, Buick Regal, a Toyota Camry or Honda Accord. And if I don't have $35,000, I will buy a 2 to 4 year old low mileage reliable used car for $12,000 such as a small Toyota, Kia or Hyundai. The lifetime savings you will realize by never buying and never leasing luxury cars is life-changing, and you aren't impressing anybody worth impressing anyway by driving a Benz or Bimmer. Yes, I partake in life's pleasures but sans brand name products, designer jeans, luxury vehicles and limited edition Rolex watches. I find ways to spend less money and achieve greater pleasure at the same time. Once you get used to it, you will realize that you can enjoy life's pleasures on a shoestring. This may sound like skimping to some people, but some status-symbol material things just do not matter to me. There are many people like me who are not materialistic. I do not live by some standard other people live by. You just have to learn to shop around and select the best value for everything. I have all the stuff I need to be happy.

Although I am low maintenance, it does not mean that I do not partake in the finer things in life. I have done quite a bit of travelling and have tasted Kaluga caviar paired with Dom Perignon. I've had Wagyu beef and whale sashimi. I can afford steaks and lobsters and I always drink wine with my dinner. I don't pay $50 per bottle. Not even $20. Not even $10. For my palate there is no big difference in the taste of wines that cost $50 and the ones that cost $8.99. Some snooty reader will probably say, "of course there is". I used to think so too in my younger days until I got a job in a company which is a subsidiary of a European company. When I worked for them, I visited Italy, Germany, France and Switzerland regularly. My European colleagues paid our U.S. branch a visit regularly also. These Swiss, Italian, German and French associates grew up on wine and beer. Most of them began drinking wine and beer with their dinners at the age of 12. They did not find any big difference in the quality and taste of the wines between the one priced at $49 and the one priced at $8.99. I like living like the rich and famous but I cannot bear throwing money away on a bottle of Dom Perignon for $400 when a Gruet for under $20 tastes just the same. A boastful scotch drinker neighbor told me once that all he drinks is the $200 a bottle Johnny Walker Blue Label Scotch because he "cannot stand the taste of cheap scotch". He agreed when I challenged him to a taste test to see if he could really tell the difference between the red label (the cheapest), black, green and blue labels. I laughed out loud when he chose the red label thinking it was the blue label. So unless there is a method to your madness, i.e. the Veblen Good you want to acquire will perhaps earn you extra income, increase your prestige or cure your depression, avoid spending money that you don't have to spend. Put that extra cash into your retirement fund if you don't know what to do with it. Don't waste your money trying to impress people. If you still have a surplus after contributing the maximum to your 401k and saving for a house, then spend it travelling to broaden your world view. Travel opens your mind and provides unique experiences to include in your "back in my day" stories to tell your grandkids.

Shop Around for Everything

Your journey towards financial independence is going to be much harder if you keep spending money that you don't have to spend. You must control spending and always find ways to reduce expenses. You must comparison shop and bargain for everything. Everything means food, toiletries, gasoline, health care, airline tickets, hotel accommodations, appliances, insurance, college education, gym membership, services, all expenses and all products great and small. An extra dollar saved here and there will accumulate over time with little notice. Comparison shopping and bargaining for everything does not necessarily mean I am being stingy. It just means I do not want to spend more than I have to, and in so doing I am on the fast track to financial independence. When I get there, I will have plenty of money to buy the things that matter to me. For now, I do not need any jewelry, expensive perfume and brand name anything. Sure designer jeans, brand name, expensive material things are nice to have, but you can really do without them at this point in your life, can't you?

Be a wise shopper not a bargain hunter. Always assess cost vs. benefit. The cheapest goods are not necessarily "the best buy". Neither are the most expensive products. If you buy a product that does not work the way it is supposed to work or the way you expected it to work; and does not last as long as it is supposed to last or as long as you expected it to last, then its cost no matter how minuscule outweighs its benefit.

Do not pay off your mortgage - Good Debt, Bad Debt

Bad debts are those that do not yield a positive return if you invested the amount you borrowed. Pay day loans, department store and credit card charges and other consumer debts are at the top of the list of bad debts since they bear high interests. But if you borrowed money at 4% APR and that money earned a return of 10% APR, that is a "good debt". And if that borrowed money generates another 1% APR on the average for the next 10 years, not only is that a "good debt" but an "excellent debt". This is exactly what happens when you have a mortgage on your principal residence. Mortgage interest payments are generally tax deductible although there are exceptions which you can check on the IRS website: https://www.irs.gov/publications/p936/ar02.html

The benefit of having a mortgage you can afford to pay should be part of your lifetime financial game plan. That is why I just don't understand why Dave Ramsey would recommend paying for your house in cash. Yes, there is a psychological element in knowing that your house is paid off but this is not a good advice in my opinion. I cringe every time I hear debt-free screamers on his radio show proclaiming "I PAID OFF MY $150,000 MORTGAGE. I AM DEBT FREEEEEE!!" I often scream back at the radio, "THAT COST YOU THOUSANDS OF DOLLARS!!!" The advice just does not make sense. There is a value to debt. The strategic use of debt is part of wealth building and a lifetime financial game plan. The profit on the spread between the cost of debt and the yield on that debt if invested can be quite substantial. If I have $280,000 in cash to use for purchasing my primary residence but the bank is willing to lend me $280,000 at 4%, 15 year fixed, I will choose to take the loan and invest the $280,000. The tax savings alone will generate a noticeable increase in take home pay. The table that follows shows the tax deductible interest on a $280,000, 4% 15 year fixed conventional mortgage. The total deductible interest for just the first 6 years is more than $56k.

Chart 11

PRINCIPAL AND INTEREST PAYMENT, 4% FIXED, 180 Mos. (15 years)

PMT NO.	PMT DATE	INTEREST @ 4.00%	PRINCIPAL	RUNNING BALANCE 280,000	INTEREST PER YEAR
1	1/10/2015	921	1,151	278,849	
2	2/10/2015	947	1,124	277,726	
3	3/10/2015	852	1,219	276,507	
4	4/10/2015	939	1,132	275,375	
5	5/10/2015	905	1,166	274,209	
6	6/10/2015	932	1,140	273,070	
7	7/10/2015	898	1,173	271,896	
8	8/10/2015	924	1,147	270,749	
9	9/10/2015	920	1,151	269,597	
10	10/10/2015	886	1,185	268,413	
11	11/10/2015	912	1,159	267,253	
12	**12/10/2015**	**879**	1,192	266,061	**10,914**
13	1/10/2016	904	1,167	264,894	
14	2/10/2016	900	1,171	263,722	
15	3/10/2016	838	1,233	262,489	
16	4/10/2016	892	1,179	261,310	
17	5/10/2016	859	1,212	260,098	
18	6/10/2016	884	1,188	258,911	
19	7/10/2016	851	1,220	257,691	
20	8/10/2016	875	1,196	256,495	
21	9/10/2016	871	1,200	255,295	
22	10/10/2016	839	1,232	254,063	
23	11/10/2016	863	1,208	252,855	
24	**12/10/2016**	**831**	1,240	251,616	**10,408**

25	1/10/2017	855	1,216	250,399	
26	2/10/2017	851	1,220	249,179	
27	3/10/2017	765	1,307	247,872	
28	4/10/2017	842	1,229	246,643	
29	5/10/2017	811	1,260	245,383	
30	6/10/2017	834	1,238	244,145	
31	7/10/2017	803	1,268	242,877	
32	8/10/2017	825	1,246	241,631	
33	9/10/2017	821	1,250	240,381	
34	10/10/2017	790	1,281	239,100	
35	11/10/2017	812	1,259	237,841	
36	**12/10/2017**	**782**	1,289	236,552	**9,790**
37	1/10/2018	804	1,268	235,284	
38	2/10/2018	799	1,272	234,013	
39	3/10/2018	718	1,353	232,659	
40	4/10/2018	790	1,281	231,379	
41	5/10/2018	761	1,310	230,068	
42	6/10/2018	782	1,290	228,779	
43	7/10/2018	752	1,319	227,460	
44	8/10/2018	773	1,298	226,161	
45	9/10/2018	768	1,303	224,859	
46	10/10/2018	739	1,332	223,527	
47	11/10/2018	759	1,312	222,215	
48	**12/10/2018**	**731**	1,341	220,874	**9,176**
49	1/10/2019	750	1,321	219,554	
50	2/10/2019	746	1,325	218,228	
51	3/10/2019	670	1,401	216,827	
52	4/10/2019	737	1,335	215,492	
53	5/10/2019	708	1,363	214,130	
54	6/10/2019	727	1,344	212,786	
55	7/10/2019	700	1,372	211,414	
56	8/10/2019	718	1,353	210,062	

57	9/10/2019	714	1,357	208,704	
58	10/10/2019	686	1,385	207,319	
59	11/10/2019	704	1,367	205,952	
60	**12/10/2019**	**677**	1,394	204,558	**8,537**
61	1/10/2020	695	1,376	203,182	
62	2/10/2020	690	1,381	201,801	
63	3/10/2020	641	1,430	200,371	
64	4/10/2020	681	1,390	198,981	
65	5/10/2020	654	1,417	197,564	
66	6/10/2020	671	1,400	196,164	
67	7/10/2020	645	1,426	194,738	
68	8/10/2020	662	1,410	193,328	
69	9/10/2020	657	1,414	191,914	
70	10/10/2020	631	1,440	190,474	
71	11/10/2020	647	1,424	189,050	
72	**12/10/2020**	**622**	1,450	187,600	**7,895**
	INTEREST				**$56,720**

The tax deduction on interest can translate to 10% to 15% of the interest amount depending on your Modified Adjusted Gross Income (MAGI) and tax bracket. The higher your tax rate is, the bigger the deduction. In the aforementioned example, 15% of $56,720 is $8,508 which is money lost forever if you do not have a $280,000 mortgage.

How to make 10% APR on borrowed money

If you take a $280,000 mortgage loan on your principal residence, the next question is where can you earn an interest of 10% APR on your $280,000 cash? You can easily make 10% APR in the stock market, see Chapter, "**ASSET ALLOCATION**..." If you saved this money due to Dave Ramsey's advice, chances are you struggled in the past few years to fully fund your 401k account. You probably contributed only a small amount into your 401k in order to save up the money to pay off your mortgage. Therefore, in the next few years you can comfortably maximize your 401k contributions since you have $280,000 cash. If you and your spouse both work and your companies offer a Roth 401k, this may be a good time to gradually convert your traditional 401k into a Roth 401k over the next few years and pay the taxes from your $280,000. You will be able to afford the maximum contribution of $18,000 a year (plus an additional $5,000 catch up if you are age 50 or over). You and your spouse can contribute $3,000 ($1500 x 2) a month immediately. Check with your company's benefit administrator or double check in the IRS website below to make sure you can contribute the maximum, https://www.irs.gov/uac/Newsroom/IRS-Announces-2016-Pension-Plan-Limitations%3B-401(k)-Contribution-Limit-Remains-Unchanged-at-$18,000-for-2016

The amount that you convert from traditional to Roth if you are under 59 ½ may be subjected to the 10% tax penalty for early withdrawal in addition to ordinary income tax. This will happen if you use any funds that you withdraw from a traditional 401k to pay the taxes on the amount you are converting. The conversion must be done correctly. Your HR benefits administrator should be able to guide you accordingly. You must pay the taxes from your after tax earnings. Also the money that you convert from traditional to Roth are restricted from withdrawal for the lesser of five years or until you reach age 59 ½. If you withdraw the converted funds from the Roth IRA prior to the date the restriction is lifted, your withdrawal will be subject to the 10% penalty.

There are two major factors to an investment strategy, your age and risk tolerance. If you have the same risk tolerance as I do and can tolerate volatility, then follow my "KISS" strategy shown in the book, "***Path2Wealth***" You will earn at least 10% APR. What is your short-term risk attitude? How much loss can you tolerate? Will 20% to 60% loss drive you crazy or are you willing to stay put and let it ride until your mutual funds recover? If you have a hard time accepting more than a 10% loss of your principal amount, then my investment system may not be right for you and historically speaking your money will earn less if you move your savings into more conservative investments such as bonds and fixed income securities. Check out your risk tolerance on this website: http://calcxml.com/calculators/inv08?skn=#top

Also google search: "risk tolerance questionnaire". If your risk tolerance is "conservative", then you are looking for less volatility. Divide 90% of your money into two or three AA+ bond funds and put the rest into a balanced fund. Volatility will be less, and though bond funds are currently earning a low return, 2% to 4% APR, you may still earn an average of 8% APR in the long run if you leave your money alone.

Do not save for an Emergency Fund – there are better ways of dealing with emergencies

INVESTOPEDIA defines an "Emergency Fund" as: "An account that is used to set aside funds to be used in an emergency, such as the loss of a job, an illness or a major expense. The purpose of the fund is to improve financial security by creating a safety net of funds that can be used to meet emergency expenses as well as reduce the need to use high interest debt, such as credit cards, as a last resort. Most financial planners suggest that an emergency fund contain enough money to cover at least six months of living expenses. Most emergency funds are highly liquid, such as checking or savings accounts. This allows quick access to funds, which is vital in emergency situations."

I myself do not have a 6-month emergency fund. I maintain a checking account with about $2000. That's it. This is the way I look at it: If I follow conventional wisdom, I will have $20,000 in my checking account earning nothing. Instead, I have the $20,000 stashed away inside my 401k account earning at least 8% a year. Using the rule of 72, savings will double approximately every 9 years (72 / Interest Rate). Chart 12 shows that my $20,000 will have grown to $43,179 in 10 years, to $93,219 in 20 and to $201,253 in 30 years. It does not make financial sense to me to lose this enormous amount of interest. Here is my strategy: Since liquidity is the key, in case of a real emergency, I will use my home equity line of credit on which I will get charged 6% APR. Or I will borrow the money I need from my 401k account at an APR of approximately 4% in today's rates.

Chart 12	
Year	Emergency Fund Amount
	20,000
1	21,600
2	23,328
3	25,194
4	27,210
5	29,387
6	31,737
7	34,276
8	37,019
9	39,980
10	43,178
11	46,633
12	50,363
13	54,392
14	58,744
15	63,443
16	68,519
17	74,000
18	79,920
19	86,314
20	93,219
21	100,677
22	108,731
23	117,429
24	126,824
25	136,970
26	147,927
27	159,761
28	172,542
29	186,345
30	201,253

Stop Wasting Food, Energy, Natural Resources

You will save a lot of money over your lifetime by conserving food, energy and natural resources. Food is one of the most basic necessities for humans and animals. Animals spend most of their waking hours hunting for food. Humans do the same although not in the same sense of the word. Many of the wars in history were fought over food. It is a shame that so much food in industrialized nations go to waste. A 2012 study by the Natural Resources Defense Council estimated that America discards up to 40% of its food, or about 20 pounds per person per month. That is the equivalent of $1500 worth of food that a family of 4 throws out each year. Food is about 13% of your budget. Take the necessary steps to minimize the waste. 1) Create a rough plan of your daily meals for a week and write down the ingredients you will need. 2) Do not buy more than a week's supply of food. 3) Avoid buying perishables in bulk. 4) Put smaller portions on your plate. This way you will not overeat or throw out what you cannot finish. 5) Reuse left overs or freeze them if you will not eat them the following day. Most people do not have any problem packing leftovers for lunch to eat at the office cafeteria the following day. 6) Take home your restaurant meal leftovers. 7) If you go to a buffet, all-you-can-eat restaurant, take only what you can finish. Do not be like jerks who pile on food on their plate, take two bites and throw the rest out.

Turn your thermostat down to 65 degrees in the winter and turn it up to 78 in the summer. Turn down your water heater thermostat to about 115 degrees. Replace all your light bulbs with LEDs or CFLs. They are expensive but they will save 90% of the cost of electricity used by regular incandescent light bulbs. Turn off lights, fans and other electrical appliances when they are not needed.

There is so much more to be said about conservation. We should realize that most of our actions impact our earth. The amount of energy we use adds greenhouse gases into the atmosphere. Our televisions, cars, gadgets and the food we eat all produce a carbon footprint. We must strive to do our part. A drop in the ocean will still make a difference.

If You Have a Pet, You Must Read This

If you don't have a pet now, don't get one unless you need it for your health and well-being. A pet is another living thing that needs tender loving care, attention and affection. It is not a toy made for your pleasure. Many animal lovers do not realize that animals prefer to be with their own kind not with humans...if they have a choice. What gives us the right to enslave another living thing, neuter or spay it, imprison it in our small apartment 10 hours a day just so we can have something to play with when we get home? If you cannot adequately provide time for your pet's companionship needs and money for your pet's expenses, please think twice about getting one. A pet, particularly a dog needs proper nutrition, training, socializing, and grooming, boarding and medical care just like other family members. It is a dependent that you cannot claim on your tax return even though you will spend a lot of money taking care of it. Yes, your dog will greet and kiss you when you come home, but believe me it is miserable the rest of its time alone and it has no say about the predicament you put it in. What do you think your dog is doing when it's all alone? It is getting tortured just waiting for you to come home. Just like other family members, you will watch your dog or cat get old, get sick and die. Only it will happen sooner than you think. So why go through this experience? Besides, in retirement don't you want the freedom to travel around without worrying about a pet?

PART III - Never Lose any of Your Savings

This Part of the book deals with strategies on preserving your savings by avoiding investment mistakes and by steering away from myths and unfounded money-making and money-savings claims that can eat away at your retirement savings.

Don't focus on taxes - Tax on retirement income, not a big deal

President Theodore Roosevelt said: "...the man of great wealth owes a particular obligation to the State because he derives special advantages from the mere existence of government"

Here is the biggest tax myth of all: "You will pay $400,000 in taxes on your $1,000,000 retirement income"

Ed Slott and many financial advisors are jumping on the "avoid taxes in retirement" bandwagon. I am in the opposite camp. Here is my thinking. I will make a lot of money on the deferred tax from my retirement account and I anticipate that money to earn an average APY of at least 10% as long as I follow my investment strategy outlined in my book, "***Path2Wealth***". But even if your money only earned a conservative 6% APY, your money will still double every 12 years using the simple Rule of 72. Therefore, I will only be too happy to take my RMDs and pay the taxes. The taxes you will pay on your retirement income will not be as bad as ***Ed Slott*** and other retirement gurus make it. See the following charts:

Chart 13

	GROSS	TAXABLE
Gross Distribution	50,000	50,000
SS	30,000	25,500
Gross Income		75,500
Federal Income Tax Using Standard Deduction		11,678
Tax as % of Gross		15.47%
Net Retirement Income		$63,822
	GROSS	TAXABLE
Gross Distribution	75,000	75,000
SS	30,000	25,500
Gross Income		100,500
Federal Income Tax Using Standard Deduction		17,928
Tax as % of Gross		17.84%
Net Retirement Income		$82,572

	GROSS	TAXABLE
Gross Distribution	100,000	100,000
SS	30,000	25,500
Gross Income		125,500
Federal Income Tax Using Standard Deduction		24,845
Tax as % of Gross		19.80%
Net Retirement Income		$100,655

	GROSS	TAXABLE
Gross Distribution	150,000	150,000
SS	30,000	25,500
Gross Income		175,500
Federal Income Tax Using Standard Deduction		38,845
Tax as % of Gross		22.13%
Net Retirement Income		$136,655

	GROSS	TAXABLE
Gross Distribution	175,000	175,000
SS	30,000	25,500
Gross Income		200,500
Federal Income Tax Using Standard Deduction		45,845
Tax as % of Gross		22.87%
Net Retirement Income		$154,655
	GROSS	TAXABLE
Gross Distribution	200,000	200,000
SS	30,000	25,500
Gross Income		225,500
Federal Income Tax Using Standard Deduction		54,017
Tax as % of Gross		23.95%
Net Retirement Income		$171,483

The charts are based on a single tax payer who takes the standard deduction. The taxes shown are only federal taxes. You should add the state and local taxes applicable to you. Many tax friendly states do not tax retirement income and SS benefits, see Chapter, "**Other Retirement Ideas**". According to the charts, if your retirement distribution plus SS pension is between $75,500 and $225,000, you will be paying federal tax of between 15.47% and 23.95%. So what? Isn't that just fair? It is not like you are being double taxed. You have not paid tax on this money before why shouldn't you pay now? Is $11,678 tax on a gross income of $75,500 really that bad? That still leaves you a net of $63,822 to live on. And if you are at the upper end of the scale with a gross retirement income of $225,500 per annum, $54,017 in federal taxes is really not that bad. You will still have $171,483 cash to live on. Moreover, if you are at this high income tax bracket, you may have other significant deductions such as mortgage interest, property taxes, medical and dental expenses, charitable contributions, state, local and sales taxes. Review the charts and choose the one that closely resembles what your retirement income will be and ask yourself if the Net Retirement Amount you will receive isn't enough. Is it worth it to fool around with setting up foundations, annuities and buying life insurance (whether term or permanent) at this point in your life? Most people's idea of retirement is to simplify their lives, i.e. less work, less worries, less stress, so why complicate your life with managing and worrying about foundations, QLAC, annuities, life insurance and other retirement schemes? Why spend extra money paying "professionals" to set up these quasi tax shelters that you don't even understand? The contracts for these instruments are so complicated that you won't even know at the end if the money you or your beneficiaries will get back is really correct. Chances are you will have to pay another professional, perhaps a lawyer, to interpret the fine print and to make sure you will end up with the right amount that you are expecting. Do the math on anything that someone is trying to sell you and you will come to the conclusion that the stress, uncertainty, complexities, commissions, mortality and expense risk charges, administrative fees, underlying fund expenses and penalties negate any tax savings you may realize.

Never Buy an Investment Property

Do not make the same mistake I made. Although being an absentee landlord sounds very appealing to many people and seems like a good idea for investing your money, it is not as easy as it seems. I had money I did not know what to do with in the late eighties so I bought a total of 8 rental townhouses one at a time in a period of 3 years. I got caught up in the rental real estate craze. Although I never had a problem with 90% of my tenants, the remaining 10% bad apples aged me quite a bit. I am sure no rational individual likes dealing with midnight calls about leaky faucets, smell of gas, broken refrigerators, pest infestations, clogged toilets, etc. etc. etc. But this is what you will be dealing with if you become a landlord. It is more work than you think. You prepare and negotiate leases, prep the property after a tenant moves out, check an applicant's credit record, collect the rent, evict tenant if tenant stops paying, spend money for necessary repairs, etc. etc. etc. The numbers do not lie. If I had only dumped my extra cash into my pot of gold, i.e. my retirement accounts instead of supporting the flat and negative cash flows of my rental properties, I would have been ahead by over $500,000.

Double Taxation on 401k Loans?

Part of my retirement game plan is to maximize my contributions to my retirement account and borrow from my retirement account in case of emergencies. So in essence I keep my "emergency fund" inside my 401k account instead of a checking account where it earns no interest. However, ***Suze Orman*** has been the loudest voice in spreading the misconception that 401k loans are double taxed. In 2006 I sent Suze Orman a private email asking her to stop saying that you will be taxed twice if you borrow money from your 401k account. This is what she wrote in one of her articles and which she often repeated in her seminars: ***"Also, never ever borrow against your 401k plan because you will pay double taxation on the money you borrow. Because you don't pay taxes on the money you put into a 401k, when you pay back the loan (which you must do within five years, or 15 years if used to buy a home), you pay it back with money you have paid taxes on. Then, when you retire and take the money out again, you end up paying taxes on it a second time."*** I explained that k-loans are not taxed twice. She never replied but I noticed that she stopped repeating this "myth" in her seminars. You did not get taxed on the money you borrowed. After you return the money you borrowed (that never got taxed), why shouldn't you get taxed (only once) when you withdraw the money for retirement? The truth is, you only get double taxed on the interest you pay, as you repay the k-loan. The interest is not a deferral as a contribution would be, so it is true you pay back the interest with after-tax dollars. Do not borrow from your 401k account unless you have to, but rest assured that 401k loans are not taxed twice.

Do not invest in anything you don't understand

In my book, ***"Path2Wealth"***, under Chapter "**Isn't There a Better Investment Strategy?**", I explain to the readers how I lost a lot of money by investing in certain investments that I did not fully understand such as: Individual Stock Picking, Day Trading, Stop Loss System, Dave Ramsey's Investment System, John Bogle's Investment Strategy and Gambling Man's Buy Low Sell High Timing System. Don't do it! Don't invest in anything you don't understand! Keep it plain and simple. You will save six million dollars and avoid lots of headaches by following my simple vanilla no frills strategy shown in Part 1.

Do Not Take Unnecessary Risks, Don't Do Anything Stupid

To make you a winner in the game of life, it is absolutely necessary to avoid doing something stupid. It also includes staying clear of dangerous situations. In the blink of an eye, doing any of the things listed on the stupid list that follows may change your life forever or worse, end it. Life in this world is so fragile. We face danger daily. There is no need to tempt fate by going out of your way looking for it. If we just follow our animal instinct of self-preservation, we can avoid a lot of dangerous situations. Even a mighty pride of lions will not attack a herd of water buffalos if the buffalos outnumber them by a lot. It is our supposed superior intelligence, emotions and thrill-seeking behavior that keep us constantly in peril. Our human intelligence is what prods us to take stupid chances and live dangerously because we think we are smart enough to overcome any peril. Sometimes we think we are smarter than we really are. We will avoid lots of dangerous situations if we just listen to our animal instinct and let it prevail over our human mental superiority. Take these as examples. If there is a war somewhere, don't take a vacation there. If there is a hurricane forecast for Florida, don't go there. If you cannot swim, don't go into deep waters. Some true to life examples of stupidity that I have read in the news: Alex Honnold climbs mountains without ropes; Michael Kennedy died playing football on skis; JFK, Jr. flew his Piper Saratoga plane at night even though he did not know how to read the plane's navigation instruments. Experts believe he experienced spatial disorientation causing his plane to crash; "Grizzly Man", Timothy Treadwell thought he could talk to bears and that they understood him. He was discovered dead and partially eaten by one of his beloved grizzlies. How about this for stupidity and thrill seeking irrational behavior: After Christopher McCandless graduated from Emory University with a double degree in History and Anthropology, he hitchhiked from South Dakota to Alaska. A hunter found his decomposing body inside a junk bus a month after he died of starvation as many authorities speculate.

An Alaskan Park Ranger Peter Christian wrote:

"When you consider McCandless from my perspective, you quickly see that what he did wasn't even

particularly daring, just stupid, tragic, and inconsiderate. First off, he spent very little time learning how to actually live in the wild. He arrived at the Stampede Trail without even a map of the area. If he [had] had a good map he could have walked out of his predicament [...] Essentially, Chris McCandless committed suicide."

I read somewhere on the internet that, "Being stupid is like being dead. Only others know it." No offense to any reader. The following is a "stupid list" I compiled as I am writing this book, and my apologies ahead of time to those who do not think that any of the following is stupid:

- Drinking and driving, texting and driving.
- Stretching out your credit card debt by making minimum monthly installments.
- Buying life insurance on your minor children.
- Ignoring a lawsuit.
- Antagonizing someone in your office who has the power to get you fired.
- Spending your entire week's salary on the lottery because the jackpot has reached $300 million.
- Claiming zero exemptions so you will receive a huge refund at the end of the year.
- Lying to the IRS, Police, FBI and CIA.
- Driving 50 miles an hour on the passing lane of a freeway.
- Stopping on a driving lane of a highway to check your tires.
- Letting your cell phone ring while on a job interview.
- Sightseeing in North Korea, Iran, Iraq and Syria.
- Jamming on your brakes to stop for a squirrel that is crossing the road.
- Shoplifting.
- Stopping 3 car lengths from the intersection while waiting for a red light to turn green.
- Sneaking into a movie house without a ticket.
- Sightseeing in North Korea, Iran, Iraq and Syria.
- Stopping your car in the middle of the road to let a baby turtle cross the street.
- Backing up your car without looking behind you.
- Sneaking out of a restaurant without paying your bill.
- Passing a school bus with flashing red lights.

- Selling your stocks after they have gone down 50%.
- Stopping your car in the middle of a railroad track to look and listen.
- Taking 2 parking spaces in a parking lot of a busy pub.
- Having unprotected sex with a stranger.
- Stopping your car and clicking your blinkers to let deer know you are giving them the right of way.
- Gambling with money that you cannot afford to lose.
- Backing up on the highway to get back to the exit you've missed.
- Taking a dip in a lake that has a sign that says, "Danger-ALLIGATORS".
- Joining a class action lawsuit to collect a $5 settlement.
- Doing drugs.
- Getting involved in a road rage argument or fight; arguing or fighting with a stranger.
- Giving your social security number, license number, bank account number to someone you don't know.
- Buying liability insurance on your rental car when it's covered by your automobile liability insurance; and buying collision damage waiver (CDW) insurance when it's covered under your credit card agreement.
- Sitting for 4 hours through a timeshare presentation to get 2 discounted Disney tickets.
- Buying a timeshare.
- Co-signing or guaranteeing someone else's loan.
- Partnering, borrowing or lending money to a relative or a friend.
- Walking in the middle of the road because car drivers will see you and avoid running over you.
- Admitting to something you did not do.
- Posting something on social media that you will be ashamed of.
- Ignoring a traffic ticket.
- Leaving just your name and phone number on an answering machine of someone who does not know you, e.g. "This is Jason. My number is 646-555-3482."
- Feeding a bear.
- Petting a bison.
- Swimming with sharks.
- Leaving a child alone with a pit bull, Doberman, Rottweiler or German shepherd.

- Running in Central Park in the dark.
- Riding a bike without a helmet.
- Disobeying the instructions of a police officer; a pilot or airline stewardess while you're on board their plane.
- Leaving your baby alone inside your car "for just a moment".
- Not using seat belts.
- Inserting your fingers into an animal's mouth to see if it will bite.
- Spending more than you make.
- Going to North Korea and stealing a banner from a North Korean hotel.
- Trying to disarm a person with a weapon.
- Parking your car and leaving your car engine running for more than 5 minutes.
- Filling your plate with food at a buffet restaurant, taking a few bites, throwing out the rest.
- Buying real estate without an attorney.
- Hiking in Iran.
- Investing your retirement money on a get-rich-quick scheme or exotic venture you don't understand.

PART IV – Protect your six million dollar pot of Gold

You can save all you want, be as stingy as Ebenezer Scrooge and you may succeed in saving $6 million for retirement, but some of your savings can simply go to waste if you fail to make sound investments and lifestyle and wealth preservation decisions. This part of the book deals with various steps you can take to safeguard and protect your pot of gold. Imagine that you spent all your working life being money-wise and prudent, then lose some of your hard earned cash in a flash. This is a real possibility no matter how smart you think you are. Most of the investors Bernie Madoff duped were banks and financial institutions managed by financial professionals. Review the following chapters and implement any of the strategies that are applicable to you.

Estate Planning, asset protection - Setting up a trust to avoid probate, exposure to creditors and predators

Estate planning goes hand in hand with asset preservation, planning for retirement and long term care. Here is a check list of things to consider as part of your estate planning package:

- **Create or update your will and living will**
  1. Take an inventory of your assets and define who will receive them and how much.
  2. Include a Living Will clause, health care declaration and a power of attorney which gives someone you choose the power to make decisions if you are mentally incapacitated. Here is an example of a living will clause, "if my physician determines that I am brain dead, any medical life support and life sustaining treatment must be terminated".
  3. Make a declaration how you want your funeral handled, e.g. "I want my body to be cremated and my ashes scattered in the Atlantic Ocean".
  4. Name a personal guardian for your minor children.
  5. Name an executor and trustee of your estate.

- **Draw up a power of attorney (POA)**
  The purpose of this important document is to give another person the authority to make important decisions on your behalf. A specific POA grants authority over a single or specific matter, whereas a general POA grants blanket authority in all matters as permitted by law. If the grantor of a POA dies or becomes incapacitated, the POA becomes invalidated. A "Durable POA" will survive the death or incapacitation of the grantor. There are do it yourself forms but it is better to consult an attorney to create a will, living will and durable power of attorney than doing it yourself. The attorney will ask you the right questions in order to find out what you want to accomplish out of these legal documents.

- **Set up a Revocable Living Trust ("RLT") to skip probate.** If you only have a will, your estate will not escape probate which is an expensive and time consuming court procedure to validate your will. If you have minor children, that is one of the best reasons you should consider setting up a Revocable Living Trust and naming the Trust as the primary or contingent beneficiary of your retirement accounts and life insurance policies. Your lawyer can set up the Trust with you and your spouse as Co-Trustees and another person as a secondary Trustee. If you and your spouse should pass away at the same time, this will enable The Secondary Trustee that you selected to accept the funds into the trust to be used in accordance with your directions, i.e. for your minor children's living expenses, schooling, etc. In the absence of a Trust, your estate will have to pass through probate and the court will have to appoint a guardian for the benefit of your minor children until they reach the age of 18. You can set up the Trust so you yourself can appoint a guardian and you can direct The Guardian what to do after your death and at what age your minor children will receive their inheritance. Even if you do not have minor children, The Trust will still serve you well by letting your estate skip probate. While you're living, you can still access and use the assets because you are the Trustee. There are many things to consider when setting up a Revocable Living Trust and an estate planning attorney should be able to readily hand you a questionnaire that will help in drafting the various provisions of the Trust. Among the many different considerations are: 1) the assets that will go into the Trust (the more assets you put into the Trust the better), 2) location of the assets (each state has different rules), 3) beneficiaries, 4) your marital status, e.g. if divorced, relationship with ex-spouses and how that may affect the Trust and beneficiaries. You can pretty much transfer into the Trust most of your assets, real estate, life insurance, patents and copyrights, jewelry, valuable works of art, stamp and coin collections, stocks and bonds, cars and even cash in the bank. The more assets there are in the Trust the better it will be for your beneficiaries when you die. The assets in the trust will pass on to your beneficiaries without probate. You can add assets to your Trust anytime and can always sell, give away or take back the assets since you are the trustee. However, a Revocable Trust will not shield your assets from frivolous lawsuits, creditors and predators. For asset protection, you will need an Irrevocable Trust.

- **Set up an Irrevocable Trust ("IT").** The purpose of setting up this type of trust is to transfer wealth, protect assets from creditor claims and frivolous lawsuits, to delay or reduce taxes, to avoid the Medicaid "spend down" provision for nursing home care. There are many different trusts for different purposes. Any mistakes in the wording of the trust will prove to be costly. A skilled and experienced trust attorney can set up an "IT" correctly once you define your objectives. Bottomline: The assets you will transfer into an "IT" are no longer yours. The assets will be protected from frivolous lawsuits, creditors and predators if you get sued but you will no longer have access to the assets. If you file for bankruptcy, the assets you transferred into the "IT" will not be counted. The assets in the trust will pass on to your beneficiaries without probate upon your death.

- **Fill out beneficiary forms to avoid probate.** Naming a beneficiary for bank accounts, 401k and brokerage accounts allows the funds to skip the probate process which can be quite lengthy. The balance of the accounts are automatically payable to the beneficiary upon your death in most states. In some states, banks require a specific beneficiary form called "payable on death (POD) beneficiary designation form". In some states, stock brokers where your investments in stocks and bonds are held, will need a specific form called Transfer on Death (TOD) form to transfer the investments to your beneficiary upon death without probate court proceedings which can be expensive.

- **Organize and store your documents and inform your executor of their location.** A simple storage system is to keep documents in a binder and put the binder inside a fireproof safe. Some of the documents you should keep in the binder are the following: Will, trusts, deeds, stock certificates, bonds, annuities, insurance policies, bank accounts, mutual funds, safe deposit box contracts, IRA and 401k account documents, credit card statements, mortgage loans, promissory notes, utilities, social security card, passport.

You need a lawyer to set up a trust and create a will. Mistakes in these documents can be costly and may result in unintended consequences for your heirs, so the legal fee a good attorney will charge is worth the price. Do you want any of your in-laws to inherit some of your assets? An estate planning attorney will give you a questionnaire that covers all bases which should answer various questions such as this one.

- **Life insurance for estate planning.** See the next chapter for a comparison between buying a life insurance policy and leaving your IRA account alone as inheritance for your heirs when you pass. Check with your tax accountant, insurance agent, financial advisor or estate tax attorney to find out if it makes sense to set up an Irrevocable Life Insurance Trust (ILIT) for your current situation. Your age, health and the size of your estate will be factors whether or not permanent life insurance makes sense for you. See the next Chapter, **"Insurance Policy vs. IRA**" for a more thorough analysis. For 90% of retirees, inheritance and estate taxes will not be an issue since $5.49 million of your estate is exempt from federal estate tax at the time of writing and many states exempt a big portion of the estate or do not have an inheritance and estate tax at all. The idea of buying life insurance at retirement is so your beneficiaries can receive the tax free life insurance proceeds upon your death and will have immediate access to cash to pay estate tax on your estate. If there is no estate tax to pay, life insurance earmarked for estate tax is not necessary. But read the next paragraph and the next chapter for additional considerations.

You must take RMDs when you reach the age of 70 ½. If you don't need the RMDs, the advice of some retirement planners is to use your RMDs to buy a universal life insurance policy to generate more wealth for your heirs. This can be accomplished by buying a standard permanent life insurance policy yourself or by setting up an irrevocable life insurance trust (ILIT) which will be the entity that will buy and own the policy. Between these two choices, setting up an ILIT to own the policy is preferred. There are many IRS rules and requirements with regard to a standard policy outside of a trust. For example, while you're still alive ownership of the policy must be completely transferred to the beneficiaries; you must relinquish control over the policy; you will have no authority to add or delete any beneficiary; policy must have been in effect three years prior to your death to be valid. The ILIT is simpler, more straight-forward and relatively inexpensive to set up. You must see a reputable retirement planner or a competent estate attorney to assess whether or not this is for you.

Insurance Policy vs. IRA, which is better for your heirs? How to protect RMDs from taxation

If you reach the age of 70 ½ and you don't need your RMDs to live on, you should begin thinking of ways of preserving your pot of gold, the money in your retirement account for your heirs. When it comes to choosing the best way of passing on your retirement assets to your beneficiaries, whether it is through a life insurance policy, traditional IRA or Roth IRA, there is no "one size fits all" solution. You have to do the math to compare all options. There are many things to consider such as your age, health, the cost of premiums, the taxes to be paid by you and by your heirs and the projected earnings of your money. To help you make a sound decision, answer the following questions:

- What is your life expectancy at 70 ½? For the sake of comparison and for the charts that follow, let's say you think you will live for another 25 years.
- What is the net amount of money your beneficiaries will receive if you die at the end of 25 years?
  - If you choose a permanent life insurance, what is the death benefit less premiums, legal fees and administrative costs? Example: You have a $500,000 IRA balance at 70 ½ which you don't need to draw on for living expenses, you can take the RMD, pay tax and immediately reinvest the after tax money. Let us suppose you are able to buy a life insurance policy with a death benefit of $950,000 for a premium of $25,000 a year. If you die after 25 years, your beneficiaries will receive the tax free insurance proceeds of $950,000 plus the after tax balance of your savings and its earnings (at 8% APY) which is calculated on Chart 14 as $1,165,510. The total after tax money you will leave your heirs will be $2,115,510. If you just kept taking the RMD, reinvested the money and paid taxes on the RMD and its earnings, after 25 years, with an average APY of 8%, the balance of your savings after taxes should be $2,499,693, see Chart 15. Your heirs will come out ahead by $384,183 if you just took the RMD, paid taxes and reinvested the after tax money. If you die only after 10 years, you will have paid less in

premiums, so the balance of your savings account will be $717,298, approximately $523,628 after taxes ($717,298 less 27% in taxes), see Chart 14b. This amount added to the death benefit of $950,000 totals $1,473,628. If you did not buy life insurance, after 10 years, the balance of your savings after taxes amounts only to $788,007 ($1,079,462 less 27% tax of $291,455). Your heirs will come out ahead by $685,621 if you bought a life insurance policy. Moreover, if your beneficiaries withdraw the full balance of $1,079,462 from your traditional IRA account in a lump sum, the tax payable will be approximately 35.6%. Your beneficiaries would only receive $695,174 net after federal income taxes. The sooner you die, the more money your beneficiaries will receive if you have an insurance policy since you will pay less in premiums. That is how insurance works.

Chart 14

SAVINGS BALANCE AFTER 25 YEARS					
If you purchase an insurance policy for an annual premium of $25,000					
Year	Age	IRA Balance	Earnings 8% APY	Insurance Premium	Net
1	70	500,000	40,000	25000	515,000
2	71	515,000	41,200	25000	531,200
3	72	531,200	42,496	25000	548,696
4	73	548,696	43,896	25000	567,592
5	74	567,592	45,407	25000	587,999
6	75	587,999	47,040	25000	610,039
7	76	610,039	48,803	25000	633,842
8	77	633,842	50,707	25000	659,549
9	78	659,549	52,764	25000	687,313
10	79	687,313	54,985	25000	717,298
11	80	717,298	57,384	25000	749,682
12	81	749,682	59,975	25000	784,657
13	82	784,657	62,773	25000	822,429
14	83	822,429	65,794	25000	863,224
15	84	863,224	69,058	25000	907,282
16	85	907,282	72,583	25000	954,864
17	86	954,864	76,389	25000	1,006,253
18	87	1,006,253	80,500	25000	1,061,754
19	88	1,061,754	84,940	25000	1,121,694
20	89	1,121,694	89,736	25000	1,186,429
21	90	1,186,429	94,914	25000	1,256,344
22	91	1,256,344	100,508	25000	1,331,851
23	92	1,331,851	106,548	25000	1,413,399
24	93	1,413,399	113,072	25000	1,501,471
25	94	1,501,471	120,118	25000	1,596,589
Estimated Tax @ 27%					431,079
Balance after tax					**$1,165,510**
Life insurance non-taxable death benefit					**$950,000**
Net cash to your heirs					**$2,115,510**

Chart 14b

IRA BALANCE AFTER 25 YEARS					
If you purchase an insurance policy for an annual premium of $25,000					
Year	Age	IRA Balance	Earnings 8% APY	Insurance Premium	Net
1	70	500,000	40,000	25000	515,000
2	71	515,000	41,200	25000	531,200
3	72	531,200	42,496	25000	548,696
4	73	548,696	43,896	25000	567,592
5	74	567,592	45,407	25000	587,999
6	75	587,999	47,040	25000	610,039
7	76	610,039	48,803	25000	633,842
8	77	633,842	50,707	25000	659,549
9	78	659,549	52,764	25000	687,313
10	79	687,313	54,985	25000	717,298
Estimated Tax @ 27%					193,671
Balance after tax					**$523,628**
Life insurance non-taxable death benefit					**$950,000**
Net cash to your heirs					**$1,473,628**

Chart 15				
SAVINGS BALANCE AFTER 25 YEARS				
Year	Age	IRA Balance	Earnings 8% APY	Net
1	71	500,000	40,000	540,000
2	72	540,000	43,200	583,200
3	73	583,200	46,656	629,856
4	74	629,856	50,388	680,244
5	75	680,244	54,420	734,664
6	76	734,664	58,773	793,437
7	77	793,437	63,475	856,912
8	78	856,912	68,553	925,465
9	79	925,465	74,037	999,502
10	80	999,502	79,960	1,079,462
11	81	1,079,462	86,357	1,165,819
12	82	1,165,819	93,266	1,259,085
13	83	1,259,085	100,727	1,359,812
14	84	1,359,812	108,785	1,468,597
15	85	1,468,597	117,488	1,586,085
16	86	1,586,085	126,887	1,712,971
17	87	1,712,971	137,038	1,850,009
18	88	1,850,009	148,001	1,998,010
19	89	1,998,010	159,841	2,157,851
20	90	2,157,851	172,628	2,330,479
21	91	2,330,479	186,438	2,516,917
22	92	2,516,917	201,353	2,718,270
23	93	2,718,270	217,462	2,935,732
24	94	2,935,732	234,859	3,170,590
25	95	3,170,590	253,647	3,424,238
Estimated Tax @ 27%				924,544
Net cash to your heirs				**$2,499,693**

- As discussed in the previous chapters, there will be RMDs on inherited IRAs and 401Ks based on the joint life expectancy of the IRA owner and beneficiary. See the tables in the IRS website, https://www.irs.gov/publications/p590b/index.html#en_US_2014_publink1000231236

- Certain assumptions are made on the preceding 25-year charts: You will pay the tax on the RMDs when due, you will immediately reinvest the RMD, your money will earn at least an APY of 8% for 25 years, the interest is compounded at least annually. Note that the 27% tax is an over estimate based on a Modified Adjusted Gross Income (MAGI) of $200,000. The tax will be higher or lower based on your actual MAGI but it will not be 40%. Many TV and radio talk show hosts play fast and loose with numbers they throw around. Do not believe "financial entertainers" who say that you will pay $400,000 tax on $1 million dollars of taxable income. First, your heirs should not make a mistake of withdrawing the full amount of the IRA they inherited in one year, thereby making the full amount taxable in one year. Second, our tax system at the time of writing is a progressive tax system. You will only pay the highest rate of 39.6% on that portion of your income that exceeds $415,050 (for tax year 2016). Click on the IRS website below to figure out your tax liability. For a single taxpayer see the following IRS chart. https://www.irs.com/articles/projected-us-tax-rates-2016

SINGLE TAXPAYER	
Taxable Income	**Tax Rate**
$0—$9,275	10%
$9,276—$37,650	$927.50 plus 15% of the amount over $9,275
$37,651—$91,150	$5,183.75 plus 25% of the amount over $37,650
$91,151—$190,150	$18,558.75 plus 28% of the amount over $91,150
$190,151—$ 413,350	$46,278.75 plus 33% of the amount over $190,150
$413,351—$415,050	$119,934.75 plus 35% of the amount over $413,350
$415,051 or more	$120,529.75 plus 39.6% of the amount over $415,050

- If you convert your traditional IRA and 401k into a Roth IRA and Roth 401k, you will have about the same after tax balance after 25 years as the traditional IRA if all the same variables (contribution amount, tax rates & APY) are used. Your guess is as good as any financial expert's on whether or not taxes and interest rates will go up.

- Is it better to give my designated beneficiaries the money now?

- If you don't need the RMDs perhaps it's wise to give your children, other relatives and charities of your choice an "early inheritance". A couple can gift $14,000 each (total of $28,000) to one single person each year without having to file a "gift tax return". Direct payments to educational or medical institutions for someone's medical bills or tuition expenses regardless of amounts do not have to be reported. Even if the gifts are in excess of the limits, you as the donor will not have to pay federal tax due to the lifetime gift exemption of $5.45 million. However, you must file a gift tax return, IRS Form 709 in any year that your gifts are in excess of the limits shown above. Direct transfers of your RMD to an eligible charitable organization are tax free. There is a maximum donation of $100,000 per annum. The transfer must be "trustee to recipient" for the donations to qualify.

SUMMARY: The concept of insurance is the same in your youth as it is in your old age as the preceding Charts 14 and 15 show. Insurance proceeds are paid in a lump sum, tax free and not subject to probate. But if you live long enough, your premium cost may exceed the amount of tax you are trying to avoid. If a retirement planner encourages the use of RMD to buy permanent life insurance, do the numbers like I did on the previous charts to make sure the figures agree with your own life expectancy and income expectations. You are the best person "to guess" how long you think you are going to live. If you have saved six million dollars at this point in your life, most of this will be a non-issue. You will simply pay the taxes and leave the after tax money to your beneficiaries.

I am myself NOT a proponent of permanent life insurance. I protect my dependents with term insurance and I make sure I do not over insure. Refer to my book, "**DynBudgTech**" for the amount of insurance you really need. Permanent life insurance is very expensive at age 70 ½. If no one except your spouse depends on you financially, you have over a million dollars in retirement savings, no mortgage and you live in a state that exempts the value of your estate from estate and inheritance taxes, I do not see the

need to buy a permanent life insurance. **Ed Slott**, CPA and PBS TV celebrity is one of the biggest proponents of whole life insurance for retirement planning. His argument is that if you die prior to your predicted life-span, the tax free proceeds from insurance is a great thing for your beneficiaries. Why, of course! That's how insurance works. He thinks that the death benefit from insurance is one of the biggest tax loopholes in taxation history because Uncle Sam does not tax insurance proceeds. But Ed Slott is not smarter than Uncle Sam and the insurance companies. Insurance companies will ALL be out of business now if all the insureds died much sooner than their predicted life span. Actuaries have a good way of figuring out how long you will live based on your age, environment, life style and other factors. As for me, I just have a weird feeling about insurance. There is something odd about having someone hope that I would have a shorter life than the predicted life-span on the life insurance policy. I would rather take the RMD, pay tax and reinvest the net amount following my investment strategy in my book, ***"Path2Wealth"***. For those of you who still feel that there is wisdom in sheltering RMD from taxation and buying whole life insurance, the article on the link below provides excellent information for creating a trust that will own the insurance policy. The article provides a lot of information for exploring Wealth Creation RMD Leverage, Irrevocable Dynasty Trust, Joint & Survivor Insurance Policy, Family Bank RMD Leverage.
http://www.investingdaily.com/18475/turning-rmd-pain-into-gain/
You will need an Estate Planning specialist with a very good reputation to implement any of these strategies. To summarize how the Trust works, 1) Your attorney will set up a Trust for you and you will name the trustee and beneficiaries, 2) You contribute your RMD to the Trust, 3) The Trustee buys a joint and survivor life insurance policy (JLS) on your life and your spouse's life using the RMD to pay for the premiums, 4) When you and your spouse pass away, the beneficiaries will receive the face value of the insurance tax free. Just like regular insurance, the sooner you pass away the greater the profit will be for the beneficiaries. That's insurance.

Paying for Long-Term Care

If you saved six million dollars for retirement, paying for long term care in a nursing home should never be an issue. LTC should not even be a problem if you only saved a million dollars for retirement. Most people do not plan on relying on Medicaid for LTC needs. The popular belief is that medical and custodial care from Medicaid providers is probably inferior since health providers who take Medicaid payments are paid a lower fee by the states (Source: Wall Street Journal https://www.wsj.com/articles/SB10001424052748704758904576188280858303612)
I do not know how true this is, but planning to rely on Medicaid, in other words, planning to go on welfare in your old age should not be part of your retirement goal. However, the cost of long term care assistance, (particularly if you and/or your spouse have to spend the rest of your life in a nursing home) can wipe out a big portion of your assets. According to the U.S. Department of Health and Human Services (HHS), about 70% of people turning 65 will need long term care services at some point in their lives. LTC is not necessarily medical care but rather custodial care which provides individuals with assistance for the Activities of Daily Living (ADLs). Custodial care is not covered by Medicare. There are 3 ways of paying for custodial care. By cash, Medicaid, or private insurance.

The following information came from Medicare.gov. Various ideas and strategies are explored towards the end of this chapter:

How can I pay for nursing home care?

There are many ways you can pay for nursing home care. Most people who enter nursing homes begin by paying for their care out-of-pocket. As you use your resources (like bank accounts and stocks) over a period of time, you may eventually become eligible for Medicaid.

Medicare generally doesn't cover long-term care stays (room and board) in a nursing home. Also, nursing home care isn't covered by many types of health insurance. However, don't drop your health care coverage (including Medicare) if you're in a nursing home. Even if it doesn't cover nursing home care, you'll need health coverage for hospital care, doctor services, and medical supplies while you're in the nursing home.

There are several other ways you can pay for nursing home care:

Personal resources

You can use your personal money and savings to pay for nursing home care. Some insurance companies let you use your life insurance policy to pay for long-term care. Ask your insurance agent how this works. When your personal resources are depleted, you will be eligible for Medicaid.

Help from your state (Medicaid)

Medicaid is a state-run program. The state laws vary with regard to income eligibility and asset requirements. Once you qualify for Medicaid, nursing home care costs, LTC and in-home care giver costs will be paid by Medicaid. Most people who want to apply for Medicaid have to reduce their assets first. There are rules about what's counted as an asset and what isn't when determining Medicaid eligibility. There are also rules that require states to allow married couples to protect a certain amount of assets and income when one of them is in an institution (like a nursing home) and one isn't. A spouse who isn't in an institution (community spouse) may keep half of the couple's joint assets, up to a maximum of $119,220 in 2015, as well as a monthly income allowance. However, some states are more generous and may allow the community spouse to keep a maximum of $100,000 in countable assets regardless of whether or not this represents half of the couple's assets. For more information, call your Medicaid office. You can also call your local Area Agency on Aging to find out if your state has any legal services where you could get more information.

Transferring assets and reducing income in order to qualify for Medicaid is not illegal. It is not unethical or immoral. It is the right thing to do if you want to preserve your lifetime savings for the benefit of your heirs....as long as you accomplish this in accordance with the law. Medicaid/Nursing Home Planning is no different from tax planning to avoid paying unnecessary taxes. Transfers of assets for less than fair market value may subject you to a penalty that Medicaid won't pay for your nursing home care for a period of time. How long the period is depends on the value of the assets you gave away. There are limited exceptions to this, especially if you have a spouse, or a blind or disabled child. Generally, giving away your assets can result in no payment for your nursing home care, sometimes for months or even years.

Federal law protects spouses of nursing home residents from losing all of their income and assets to pay for nursing home care for their spouse. When one member of a couple enters a nursing home and applies for Medicaid, his or her eligibility is determined under "spousal impoverishment" rules. Spousal impoverishment helps make sure that the spouse still at home will have the money needed to pay for living expenses by protecting a certain amount of the couple's resources, as well as at least a portion of the nursing home resident's income, for the use of the spouse who is still at home. For more information, call your Medicaid office. To apply for Medicaid, call your Medicaid office. They can tell you if you qualify for the Medicaid nursing home benefit or other programs, such as the Programs of All-Inclusive Care for the Elderly (PACE), or home and community-based waiver programs.

Not all nursing homes accept Medicaid payments. Check with the nursing home to see if they accept people with Medicaid, and if they have Medicaid beds available. You may be eligible for Medicaid coverage in a nursing home even if you haven't qualified for other Medicaid services in the past. Sometimes you won't be eligible for Medicaid until you've spent some of your personal resources on medical care. You may be moved to another room in the Medicaid-certified section of the nursing home when your care is paid by Medicaid. To get more information on Medicaid eligibility requirements in your state, call your Medicaid office.

You may have to pay out-of-pocket for nursing home care each month. The nursing home will bill Medicaid for the rest of the amount. How much you owe depends on your income and deductions.

Long-term care and residential care have categories of different care levels. Generally, Medicaid will pay the bill for eligible seniors.

Table 16 shows a comparison of different care facilities and their approximate costs which were in effect at the time of writing:

Chart 16

HOUSING OPTION	PURPOSE	APPROX. COST
Assisted Living	For people who need help with both simple and complex ADLs	$7000/MO. Medicaid for eligible seniors and low income individuals
Board and Care Homes	People who need help with complex ADLs	$4500/MO. Medicaid for eligible seniors and low income individuals
Skilled Care Facilities	For people with significant short-term care needs	$7500/MO. Medicaid for eligible seniors and low income individuals Medicare usually covers for 20 days if medically necessary
Long-Term Care Facility	For people who will not return to independent living	$90000/PER YEAR covered by Medicaid and long-term care insurance

The state cannot put a lien on your home if there is a reasonable chance you will return home after getting nursing home care or if you have a spouse or dependents living there. This means they cannot take, sell or hold your property to recover benefits that are correctly paid for nursing home care while you are living in a nursing home in this circumstance. In most cases, after a person who gets Medicaid nursing home benefits passes away, the state must try to get whatever benefits it paid for that person back from their estate.

However, they cannot recover on a lien against the person's home if it is the residence of the person's spouse, brother or sister (who has an equity interest and was residing in the home at least one year prior to the nursing home admission), or a blind or disabled child or a child under the age of 21 in the family.

Long-term care (LTC) insurance

This type of private insurance policy can help pay for many types of long-term care, including both skilled and non-skilled care. LTC insurance can vary widely. Some policies may cover only nursing home care. Others may include coverage for a whole range of services like adult day care, assisted living, medical equipment, and informal home care. If you have LTC insurance, check your policy or call the insurance company to find out if the care you need is covered. If you are shopping for long-term care insurance, find out which types of long-term care services and facilities the different policies cover. Also, check to see if your coverage could be limited because of a pre-existing condition. Make sure you buy from a reliable company that's licensed in your state. Federal employees, members of the uniformed services, retirees, their spouses, and other qualified relatives may be able to buy LTC insurance at discounted group rates. Get more information about LTC insurance for federal employees from this website:
https://www.opm.gov/healthcare-insurance/long-term-care/

SUMMARY:

- Medicare does not cover medical services for cognitive ailments like dementia, or simply because you are unable to handle some of the basic activities of daily living like eating, drinking, walking, dressing, bathing and grooming. A full time caregiver for in-home assistance will cost approximately $230 a day in 2016 dollars.
- Long term care in a nursing home will cost approximately $90,000 a year in 2016 dollars. The average nursing home stay is about 3 years.
- Medicare covers 100% of nursing care in a nursing home, board and care convalescent centers, or in-home care but only for 20 days and only if medically necessary following a hospital stay of more than three days. It will also pay for physical therapy, wheelchairs, walkers, hospital beds and even hospice care for those with less than six months to live.

Exploring different strategies in dealing with LTC expenses

It would be great if we can choose how to die and when to die. As it is, we have to explore the few options available to us. According to statistics shown below, only 31% of us will die never needing long term care. Private LTC insurance is very expensive. You cannot buy insurance only when you need it. Even if you are in good health, the older you get the more the premiums would cost. Estimated Years of needing Long-Term Care after turning Age 65:

More than 5 years 20%
2 to 5 years 20%
1 to 2 years 12%
1 year or less 17%
None 31%

If you are in good health, take care of yourself and are feeling confident that you will be among the 31% who will never need LTC, then you can take a chance and do nothing. The worst case scenario if you go by the statistics is you will spend $230 a day (in 2016 dollars) for 5 years for a total of $419,750 in today's dollars. Remember this is only for one person. After spending down your cash, the state government will take care of you through the Medicaid program.

At age 50, long-term care may not be something that you are thinking about. But premiums are a lot cheaper at 50 than at 65 or at 70. At age 70, the premiums will be so much more expensive and you will be subjected to a rigorous underwriting process which may include urine and blood tests and cognitive testing such as memory recall, reasoning and basic math. 45% of applicants 70 years and older are declined. If you are healthy and never smoked, at 50 you can buy a guaranteed renewable policy for about $1500 per annum. In most states your premiums will be subject to rate increases as you grow older. Your LTC premiums may increase to such an unaffordable level when you need the insurance most. But even if the premium never increased you will still spend at least $60,000 in premiums over 40 years. That is $120,000 for a couple. If you factor in the interest that money could have earned over 40 years, using the rule of 72 where your money doubles every 10 years or so, that is a cash outlay of over $400,000 per person by the time you reach

90. You may die without ever needing LTC. At 65, the premiums for a renewable policy, if you are in good health could be about $2500 per annum. You will spend $62,500 in premiums if you live to be 90. That is $125,000 for a couple without factoring in the interest the premium payments could have earned. You may never need long-term care. Typical initial policies are shown on the following two charts:

State	NJ
Birthdate	1/2/1966
Age	50
Facility Daily Benefit	$300
Facility Benefit Period	3 Years
Home Care Daily Benefit	100%
Monthly Home Care	Monthly
Elimination Period	0 Days
Marital Discount	Both Insured
Payment Option	Annual
Gender	Male
Monthly Benefit	$9,000
Maximum	$324,000
Assisted Living	100%
Cash Benefit	30%
Cash Benefit Amount	$2,400
Premium	$1,500

State	NJ
Birthdate	1/2/1951
Age	65
Facility Daily Benefit	$300
Facility Benefit Period	3 Years
Home Care Daily Benefit	100%
Monthly Home Care	Monthly
Elimination Period	0 Days
Marital Discount	Both Insured
Payment Option	Annual
Gender	Male
Monthly Benefit	$9,000
Maximum	$324,000
Assisted Living	100%
Cash Benefit	30%
Cash Benefit Amount	$2,400
Premium	$2,500

My LTC Strategy

Since my health and longevity are big unknowns, I prefer the flexibility of not losing a penny on insurance premiums if I never need long-term care. So my preference is to deposit the money I would have paid for LTC insurance into my Roth 401k, sort of self-insurance. If it earns an APR of 8%, I will have $454,865 if I started at 50 until I reach 90 years of age and $215,877 if I started at 65. See the following charts:

Age	Premiums $1500/year	Interest	Total Savings
50	1,500	120	1,620
51	3,120	250	3,370
52	4,870	390	5,259
53	6,759	541	7,300
54	8,800	704	9,504
55	11,004	880	11,884
56	13,384	1,071	14,455
57	15,955	1,276	17,231
58	18,731	1,499	20,230
59	21,730	1,738	23,468
60	24,968	1,997	26,966
61	28,466	2,277	30,743
62	32,243	2,579	34,822
63	36,322	2,906	39,228
64	40,728	3,258	43,986
65	45,486	3,639	49,125
66	50,625	4,050	54,675
67	56,175	4,494	60,669
68	62,169	4,974	67,143
69	68,643	5,491	74,134
70	75,634	6,051	81,685
71	83,185	6,655	89,840

72	91,340	7,307	98,647
73	100,147	8,012	108,159
74	109,659	8,773	118,432
75	119,932	9,595	129,526
76	131,026	10,482	141,508
77	143,008	11,441	154,449
78	155,949	12,476	168,425
79	169,925	13,594	183,519
80	185,019	14,802	199,820
81	201,320	16,106	217,426
82	218,926	17,514	236,440
83	237,940	19,035	256,975
84	258,475	20,678	279,153
85	280,653	22,452	303,105
86	304,605	24,368	328,974
87	330,474	26,438	356,912
88	358,412	28,673	387,085
89	388,585	31,087	419,672
90	421,172	33,694	454,865

Age	Premiums $2500/year	Interest	Total Savings
65	2,500	200	2,700
66	5,200	416	5,616
67	8,116	649	8,765
68	11,265	901	12,167
69	14,667	1,173	15,840
70	18,340	1,467	19,807
71	22,307	1,785	24,092
72	26,592	2,127	28,719
73	31,219	2,498	33,716
74	36,216	2,897	39,114
75	41,614	3,329	44,943
76	47,443	3,795	51,238
77	53,738	4,299	58,037
78	60,537	4,843	65,380
79	67,880	5,430	73,311
80	75,811	6,065	81,876
81	84,376	6,750	91,126
82	93,626	7,490	101,116
83	103,616	8,289	111,905
84	114,405	9,152	123,557
85	126,057	10,085	136,142
86	138,642	11,091	149,733
87	152,233	12,179	164,412
88	166,912	13,353	180,265
89	182,765	14,621	197,386
90	199,886	15,991	215,877

****

The money is mine if I never need LTC. I will invest the money inside my 401k account following my strategy in the book, ***"Path2Wealth"***. My money should earn at least 8% APY.

- **How to qualify for Medicaid benefits for LTC**

Monthly income and countable assets are two determining factors for Medicaid benefit eligibility. As of the time of writing, an applicant cannot earn more than $2199 per month and must not have more than $2000 in countable assets. When your countable assets are down to $2000, Medicaid will take over. Some assets are exempt from valuation such as the value of your home if it is $500,000 or less (some states have a higher exemption limit), your car with a value of $4500 or less, funeral burial funds of $1500, personal property that is essential to self-support and life insurance. Not all nursing homes and home health care providers accept Medicaid. In some cases, you may be moved to another room in a Medicaid-certified section of the same facility. Medicare.gov states, "The state cannot put a lien on your home if there is a reasonable chance you will return home after getting nursing home care or if you have a spouse or dependents living there. This means they cannot take, sell, or hold your property to recover benefits that are correctly paid for nursing home care while you are living in a nursing home in this circumstance. In most cases, after a person who gets Medicaid nursing home benefits passes away, the state must try to get whatever benefits it paid for that person back from their estate. But they cannot recover on a lien against the person's home if it's the residence of the person's spouse, brother or sister (who has an equity interest and was residing in the home at least one year prior to the nursing home admission), or a blind or disabled child or a child under the age of 21 in the family."

- Transferring assets to qualify for Medicaid.

There is a 60-month "look back" period for transfers made after February 8, 2006. Many people do not transfer any of their assets to their heirs until they are faced with the sad reality that they need to go to a nursing home. It is human nature that given the choice, you would rather give your money to your children (let the government take care of you) than give it to the nursing home. The government knows this that is why "the penalty period" was established when the Deficit Reduction Act of 2005 (DRA) was enacted. The penalty applies for transfers made within 60 months from the date that transferor moved to a nursing home and had applied and been approved for Medicaid if not for the transfer. You will be eligible for Medicaid if your total cash in the bank is less than $2000. Medicaid will not pay during the length of the penalty period which is calculated by dividing the amount of transfer by the average cost of nursing home care in your state. The penalty period begins after Medicaid approves your application. If the amount of transfer was $75,000 and average cost of monthly nursing home care in your state is $7500, the penalty period is 10 months, i.e. $75,000/$7500. The chart that follows illustrates the timetable for a person who has $2,000 or more in savings:

AMOUNT OF TRANSFER	$75,000
MONTHLY NURSING HOME RATE	$7,500
PENALTY PERIOD ($75000/$7500)	10 Months
Admitted to nursing home	1/2/2016
	2/2/2016
	3/2/2016
	4/2/2016
	5/2/2016
Applied for Medicaid	6/2/2016
	7/2/2016
	8/2/2016
Spent savings down to less than $2000	9/2/2016
	10/2/2016
Approved by Medicaid	11/2/2016
10-Month Penalty starts	12/2/2016
	1/2/2017
	2/2/2017
	3/2/2017
	4/2/2017
	5/2/2017
	6/2/2017
	7/2/2017
	8/2/2017
	9/2/2017
10-Month Penalty ends, Medicaid pays from this date	10/2/2017

The reader who is paying attention will probably ask, "Well, who will pay the nursing home bills from January 2, 2016 through October 2, 2017?" The answer is you are responsible for the bills not the person you transferred the money to unless that person signed the admission agreement as a "responsible party" or "guarantor". The nursing home's collection agency will go after you not the transferee. Most people want to do the right thing so the practical solution is for the transferee to voluntarily return the $75,000 as payment towards the nursing home bills. Another timetable follows. This is if the Medicaid applicant has no more than $2000 in countable assets. The applicant applies immediately upon admission to the nursing home:

AMOUNT OF TRANSFER	$75,000
MONTHLY NURSING HOME RATE	$7,500
PENALTY PERIOD ($75000/$7500)	10 Months

Admitted to nursing home, countable assets not more than $2000 & immediately applied for Medicaid	1/2/2016
	2/2/2016
Approved by Medicaid	3/2/2016
10-Month Penalty starts	4/2/2016
	5/2/2016
	6/2/2016
	7/2/2016
	8/2/2016
	9/2/2016
	10/2/2016
	11/2/2016
	12/2/2016
	1/2/2017
10-Month Penalty ends, Medicaid pays from this date	2/2/2017

- **Permitted transfers.** The following information was published and is available on the website, Medicaid.gov:
  While most transfers are penalized with a period of Medicaid ineligibility of up to five years, certain transfers

are exempt from this penalty. Even after entering a nursing home, you may transfer any asset to the following individuals without having to wait out a period of Medicaid ineligibility:

• Your spouse (but this may not help you become eligible since the same limit on both spouse's assets will apply).

• Your child who is blind or permanently disabled.

• Into trust for the sole benefit of anyone under age 65 and permanently disabled.

• In addition, you may transfer your home to the following individuals (as well as to those listed above):

• Your spouse.

• Your child who is under age 21.

• Your child who has lived in your home for at least two years prior to your moving to a nursing home and who provided you with care that allowed you to stay at home during that time.

• A sibling who already has an equity interest in the house and who lived there for at least a year before you moved to a nursing home.

How to reduce income to qualify for Medicaid

If your income exceeds the eligibility threshold, which at the time of writing is $2199 a month, the best thing to do is to consult a Medicaid Planning professional or an Elder Care attorney to set up a Qualified Income Trust (QIT) such as an Income Cap Trust, Miller Trust or a Pooled Income Trust that you can contribute into thereby reducing your income. As an example, if you receive $1500 from SSA and $1500 from other sources, $801 will be deposited into the QIT to exclude it from your monthly income, thereby qualifying you for Medicaid benefits. Every month your trustee will have to use the money in the QIT to pay for your care including turning the available amount to the nursing home or assisted living facility. Medicaid pays the rest of your expenses. Upon your death, the state is entitled to reimbursement from the money left in the QIT. Medicaid laws are complex and they vary from state to state. This is not a do-it-yourself project. You need a lawyer to set up a QIT. Maybe you will spend $2000 to $7,000 on legal fees to set up a QIT for the less complicated ones, but you will qualify for Medicaid if the trust is done correctly.

Creative Ways of Hiding Assets to Qualify for Medicaid

The following are other strategies that I do not endorse. They are included in this book for entertainment only. In fact, some of these egregious activities may land you in jail. But it is a fact some people have been employing these tactics to qualify for Medicaid. I learned about these activities when I interviewed some retirees who have gone through the experience. One retiree who shall remain nameless said, "There is a fine line between right and wrong, between legal and illegal." Another retiree said, "It's only illegal if you get caught". Yet another retiree said, "as long as in my mind I am telling the truth, I have no guilt and I have not perjured myself. The government has nothing on me". I discovered these are some of the ways some retirees hide cash from Medicaid:

- **In a bank's safe deposit box** – This will sound like a strange story to some people, but this happens more often than you think. A retiree by the name of Perry D (not his real name) lives in California. He and his wife are counting on Medicaid for their LTC. Between the two of them, they receive about $3500 a month in SS benefits which they will have to turn over to the nursing home in return for long term care if the need arises. Medicaid covers anything Medicare does not cover such as long term nursing care, assisted living facility and custodial care (home health care). He and his wife are both 70 years old and they keep $185,000 cash in 2 safe deposit boxes in two different banks. Perry is a law school drop-out so he knows a little about the law. He tells me that keeping money in a safe deposit box is perfectly legal as long as the money is not ill-gotten. Perry and his wife are in marginal health. Both are diabetics and are worried that they might need LTC in a nursing home or may have to move into an assisted living facility in a few years. Their house with a market value of $380,000 is all paid for. Their two children are included in the deed as joint tenants with their parents with right of survivorship and they use the house "officially" as their principal residence. Perry and his wife lease their 2 cars and have no other countable assets except for the $185,000 cash hidden in the safe deposit boxes. Multiple persons can be named as lessees so he has his name, his wife and two children on the rental agreements although they did not give their children keys to the boxes. Yes Perry admits he could be earning at least 1% interest on this money but he is more worried about having to turn over the money to the health provider when the time comes if it's not hidden. As a precaution, he drafted the following sworn affidavit which he keeps with the money:

Affidavit and Certification

This is to certify that we gifted the following amounts to our children:

1/2/2003	$11,000	John D	SS# ***-**-4156
	$11,000	Susan D	SS# ***-**-4157
1/2/2004	$11,000	John D	SS# ***-**-4156
	$11,000	Susan D	SS# ***-**-4157
1/2/2005	$11,000	John D	SS# ***-**-4156
	$11,000	Susan D	SS# ***-**-4157
1/2/2006	$12,000	John D	SS# ***-**-4156
	$12,000	Susan D	SS# ***-**-4157
1/2/2007	$12,000	John D	SS# ***-**-4156
	$12,000	Susan D	SS# ***-**-4157
1/2/2008	$12,000	John D	SS# ***-**-4156
	$12,000	Susan D	SS# ***-**-4157
1/2/2009	$13,000	John D	SS# ***-**-4156
	$13,000	Susan D	SS# ***-**-4157
1/2/2010	$13,000	John D	SS# ***-**-4156
	$13,000	Susan D	SS# ***-**-4157
	$190,000		

Affiants' Signatures: Perry D ____________________,
Mrs. Perry D, ______________

Subscribed and sworn to before me this __________
day of ___________,20xx , City, County, State.

Notary Public

Perry told me that he has never encountered a problem. Except for the loss of 1% to 2% annual interest, he is happy with what he is doing. He thinks that if he and his wife ever need LTC, which can be any day now, Medicaid will take care of them. They will tell the absolute truth that they have no cash in the bank and that they did not make any transfers of cash within the 60-month look back period. Of course they have to watch that the balances of their individual checking accounts under their separate names do not go over $2000 each. They withdraw their social security benefit payments (about $1750 each) immediately upon receipt, spend the money to maintain their daily needs and lifestyle, then put the remaining cash, if any, into the safe deposit boxes. Perry gave me more details. The Affidavit does not have to be backdated since the affiant is merely attesting to what happened in the past. Perry and his wife did not withdraw large amounts of cash from their savings. Over 5 years ago, they withdrew $5000 a month or less over the course of three years which they systematically transferred into the safe deposit boxes. Perry tells me that the money keeps growing. They do not spend that much money on their daily needs so they always have something extra to put into the safety deposit boxes at the end of the month. They will need to update the affidavit as needed.

- **In a foreign bank account** – A retiree by the name of Jesse H is 68 years old. He and his wife live in Illinois. They receive $2000 each monthly from the SSA. They crossed the Canadian border 5 years ago and opened an account at a TD bank in Windsor, Ontario. The account is a "joint account" with their 3 daughters. He tells me they only had to show two IDs, their passports and credit cards. They opened the interest bearing savings account, no other questions asked. They systematically transferred their liquid assets totaling the equivalent of CAN$390,000 into the account. They told the bank they are planning to buy a house in Ontario and needed a place to park their money. At the end of the year, the bank sends them a T5NR slip for the 10% withholding tax on the interest the money earned. This is the counterpart of IRS form 1099INT but the T5NR slip makes no reference to any U.S. taxpayer's SS number because this form is for non-residents. Since ¾ of the money in the account legally belongs to their daughters, in the beginning of the year Jesse asks his three daughters this question, "Will you gift your mother and me $10,000 each?" Their daughters always say yes, so they are allowed to withdraw up to CAN$60,000 ($10,000x3x2) if they need it and not have to worry about their daughters having to file a gift tax return. Last year they took some money out and went on a 130-day world cruise. With regard to the requirement to file IRS Form 8938, Statement of Specified Foreign Financial Assets, Jesse tells me they are not required to file since together with their daughters and their spouses they do not satisfy the reporting threshold of more than US$100,000 per married couple in foreign assets. I've interviewed other retirees who have hidden bank accounts in foreign countries such as India, Malaysia, Indonesia, Italy, Germany, The Bahamas, and many other Caribbean and South American Countries. Most of the people I've interviewed who hold foreign bank accounts claim that they comply with IRS regulations shown on the link below.

https://www.irs.gov/businesses/small-businesses-self-employed/report-of-foreign-bank-and-financial-accounts-fbar

- **In a fire proof safe** – This is the story of Hazel J, a 72 year old widow retiree. She does not think she has enough money to be concerned about as other retirees. She lives in Washington State. She has 3 adult children but they live far away from her. Her 2 bedroom condo is fully paid for and has a market value of $280,000. She added her children as co-owners of the condo more than 5 years ago. As a precaution she signed an affidavit stating "It is my intention to return home after my discharge from the hospital or any nursing home and/or health care facility..." Her cash on hand is less than $100,000 and her SS benefit is around $1800 a month. She has been in and out of nursing homes in the past two years, the expenses all paid by Medicare and Medicaid. First she had a hip replacement. After 20 weeks at a rehab center she was transferred to an assisted living facility. When she applied for Medicaid assistance, she told the authorities that she has no countable assets. She tells me that the $100,000 cash hidden in her vault does not belong to her but to her children and grandchildren. She withdraws money from that vault only with the permission of her children and grandchildren when they want to give her some money. After she got well and was able to take care of ADLs, she returned home. She still needed custodial care 3 times a week at home which Medicaid paid for. After a year or so, she needed knee surgery and the process started all over again. Right now she is looking to get into an assisted living facility. All through her retired life, she keeps her cash in a fire proof safe deposit box dropped into a secret vault underneath the concrete floor of her garage. Her cash is in denominations of $20s, $50s and $100s. She tells me that she takes extra precaution by wrapping the money in zip lock bags to protect it from moisture. She has been doing this since her husband died a few months after she retired at 66.

- **In a domestic S. Corporation, Limited Liability Corporation (LLC) or Partnership** – Adam H and his wife are both 70 years old. In their early 60s, they asked their lawyer to set up an LLC. The membership units of the LLC are owned by an irrevocable trust that the lawyer set up simultaneously. They transferred most of their liquid assets to this LLC. If they ever need LTC, they can apply for Medicaid and will likely get approved since Medicaid will not find assets under their names and social security numbers. Adam tells me this is perfectly legal as part of estate planning. Adam adds, this is not a do it yourself undertaking. You will need a lawyer to create an estate plan since the provisions of the plan can be complex. One of the most important provisions of the plan is to define the conditions under which the funds may be withdrawn. The funds in the Trust are no longer yours once you turn them over to the Trust. But you and your spouse will qualify for Medicaid. The cost of creating a plan is approximately $2,000 to $10,000 depending on how simple or complex the plan is.

- **In a Life Estate** – Rachel, a 69 year old widow told me this story. She has no immediate family members. Her only income is her social security pension of $1900 a month. She owns a fully paid for house that is valued at $300,000. She has no immediate family members but she has friends who live close by and she loves the neighborhood. She would never dream of moving anywhere else. She can no longer afford the real estate taxes and maintenance on the property. So she donated her house to a 501(c) nonprofit corporation. The corporation's lawyer set up a life estate whereby Rachel can live in the house for as long as she lives. In return, the corporation which now owns the house provides necessary maintenance and the property is now exempt from real estate taxes. Rachel qualifies for Medicaid. She tells me that you need a lawyer to set up a Life Estate. You cannot do this on your own.

Other Retirement Ideas

- **Moving to retirement friendly states**

You have greater flexibility on how to spend your retirement years if you are in good health, with good mobility and very little restriction on your diet. If you have no health issues that compel you to favor one state over another, you can move to states that are friendly for retirees, or to other countries that are viable. When I retire I will consider moving to a state that has great year round weather, easy access to good health care, a low crime rate, low income tax, sales tax and property tax rates, low insurance rates and low cost of living. Since salt water fishing is what I hope to be doing every day of my retired life, I want to be close to the gulf, ocean or sea. Others may want to live close to the mountains, golf courses, biking and hiking trails.

According to CNN and the U.S. News and World Report, the states chosen in 2016 with a combination of favorable factors were Florida, Texas, Nevada, Colorado, Washington State, South Carolina, South Dakota, Utah, Idaho, Wyoming, New Mexico, Montana, Delaware, Arizona and New Mexico. Bankrate.com has a different rating system which combines only a variety of statistics, i.e. cost of living, crime rate, health care quality, weather and well-being. The rankings for the year 2015 are shown on the following chart:

Chart 21

Rank	State	Cost of living	Crime rate	Community well-being	Health care	Tax rate	Weather
1	Wyoming	18	5	5	32	3	8
2	South Dakota	26	11	6	9	2	29
3	Colorado	32	25	4	13	16	3
4	Utah	15	22	8	11	30	6
5	Virginia	20	4	17	14	24	10
6	Montana	33	19	3	27 (tied)	13	9
7	Idaho	2	2	36	38	22	7
8	Iowa	13	12	14	6	20	39
9	Arizona	27	41	9	21	15	5
10	Nebraska	14	20	20	15	21	21
11	Maine	38	3	22	3	37	27
12	North Dakota	29	10	15	12	18	43
13	Wisconsin	25	13	13	2	47	46
14	Minnesota	30	15	7	5	42	48
15	New Hampshire	39	7	21	1	7	49
16	North Carolina	21	33	23	16	31	19
17	Kansas	8	32	25	36	28	17

35	Washington	36	36	24	17	25	40
36	Ohio	16	27	47	30	32	37
37	Indiana	3	30	46	39	27	34
38	Missouri	12	37	45	35	23	38
39	California	49	31	10	41	45	2
40	New Jersey	43	8	32	18	48	15
41	Maryland	40	34	34	19	44	13
42	Connecticut	46	6	18	25	49	14
43	Alaska	47	46	2	37	1	50
44	Oklahoma	4	40	48	50	11	26
45	Hawaii	50	26	1	22	36	32
46	Louisiana	19	49	42	49	5	44
47	Arkansas	11	45	44	45	34	30
48	Oregon	44	28	31	34	40	31
49	West Virginia	35	14	50	44	33	47
50	New York	48	17	40	31	50	25

The preceding chart ranks each state using six categories chosen when weighted equally. The statistics for various locations within each state may vary widely. Many states allow various jurisdictions (counties) within their state to add local sales taxes. In addition cost of living, health care, crime rate and weather can vary from city to city. Here are my personal favorite retirement cities. My desire to be close to salt water has been taken into consideration. If you have other interests such as golfing, tennis, theatre, museums, cultural events, biking, hiking and mountain climbing, my choices may not agree with yours:

- **Top Retirement Cities:**
  Punta Gorda, Cape Coral and Port Charlotte, Florida; Dauphin Island and Gulf Shores, Alabama; Long Beach, Gulport, Ocean Springs and Biloxi, Mississippi; Port Arthur and Rockport, Texas; Myrtle Beach and Charleston, South Carolina; Dewey and Bethany Beach, Delaware; Portland, Eugene and Medford, Oregon; Ocean City and Belmar, NJ.

  After family and friends, I consider good climate, availability of good health care and low crime rate as the primary reasons for choosing a retirement location. State income tax on retirement income and social security benefits, sales taxes, property taxes, car taxes, various fees, tolls, insurance rates and cost of living tend to balance themselves out. So to me, these are secondary factors. If one tax is lower in a certain jurisdiction, another type of tax is higher to offset it. How else can they run their state governments if all types of taxes are equally low? The cost of insurance and the cost of living are also balancing factors in most locations. Take Florida as an example. It has no state income tax but sales taxes, property taxes and home insurance premiums are high.

  However, estate and inheritance tax is a deal breaker for many retirees who have accumulated millions of dollars in savings. As of the time of writing, here is the list of the jurisdictions that do not impose a state estate tax or a state inheritance tax:

  1. Alabama
  2. Alaska
  3. Arizona
  4. Arkansas
  5. California
  6. Colorado
  7. Florida
  8. Georgia
  9. Idaho
  10. Indiana
  11. Kansas

12. Louisiana
13. Michigan
14. Mississippi
15. Missouri
16. Montana
17. Nevada
18. New Hampshire
19. New Mexico
20. North Carolina
21. North Dakota
22. Ohio
23. Oklahoma
24. South Carolina
25. South Dakota
26. Texas
27. Utah
28. Virginia
29. West Virginia
30. Wisconsin
31. Wyoming

Here is the list of jurisdictions that collect a state estate tax or a state inheritance tax at the time of writing:

Connecticut - estate tax and gift tax
Delaware - estate tax
District of Columbia - estate tax
Hawaii - estate tax
Illinois - estate tax
Iowa - inheritance tax
Kentucky - inheritance tax
Maine - estate tax
Maryland - estate tax and inheritance tax
Massachusetts - estate tax
Minnesota - estate tax
Nebraska - inheritance tax
New Jersey - estate tax and inheritance tax
New York - estate tax
Oregon - estate tax
Pennsylvania - inheritance tax
Rhode Island - estate tax
Tennessee - estate tax

Vermont - estate tax
Washington - estate tax

Please remember that tax laws change and the preceding information may no longer be current. Reform and repeal of estate and inheritance taxes have been frequent in various states in the last few years. Check on the website below for updated information:
http://wills.about.com/od/stateestatetaxes/fl/States-Without-an-Estate-Tax-or-an-Inheritance-Tax-in-2015.htm

Another website that is full of important resources is,

https://smartasset.com/retirement/retirement-taxes

This website has an interactive retirement calculator, 401k calculator, SS calculator, retirement state tax friendliness calculator, home buying calculator and many more. Here are the "tax friendliness" ranking of each state from this website:

Very Tax Friendly
States that either have no state income tax, no tax on retirement income, or a significant tax deduction on retirement income. In addition, states in this category have friendly sales, property, estate and inheritance tax rates.
Alaska
Florida
Georgia
Mississippi
Nevada
South Dakota
Wyoming

Tax Friendly
States that do not tax Social Security income and offer an additional deduction on some or all other forms of retirement income. Generally, states in this category also have relatively friendly sales, property, estate, inheritance and income tax rates.
Alabama
Arkansas

Colorado
Delaware
Idaho
Illinois
Kentucky
Louisiana
Michigan
New Hampshire
Oklahoma
Pennsylvania
South Carolina
Tennessee
Texas
Virginia
Washington
West Virginia

Moderately Tax Friendly

States that offer smaller deductions on some or all forms of retirement income. The sales, property, estate, inheritance and income tax rates in this category range in friendliness based on the degree of retirement deductions available.

Arizona
District of Columbia
Hawaii
Indiana
Iowa
Kansas
Maryland
Massachusetts
Missouri
Montana
New Jersey
New Mexico
New York
North Carolina
North Dakota
Ohio
Oregon
Utah
Wisconsin

Not Tax Friendly

States that offer minimal to no retirement income tax benefits. These states also do not have particularly friendly sales, property, estate and inheritance tax rates.

California
Connecticut
Maine
Minnesota
Nebraska
Rhode Island
Vermont

- **Moving to retirement friendly foreign locations**

If you can get past moving away from relatives, friends and acquaintances, many retirees become perfectly content living in foreign countries where the climate is great, good quality health care is cheap and the cost of living is half of that in America. U.S. News and World Report and International Living Magazine consistently rank these foreign locations at the top of their list: Santa Fe and Panama City, Panama; Belize; Medellin, Colombia; Vilcabamba and Cuenca, Ecuador; Granada and San Juan del Sur, Nicaragua; Cuepos and San Jose, Costa Rica; La Cieba and Trujillo, Honduras; Buenos Aires, Argentina; La Serena and Viña del Mar, Chile; San Miguel de Allende, Campeche, Puerto Vallarta and Guadalajara, Mexico; Costa del Sol and Estepona, Spain; Algarve and Lisbon, Portugal; Phuket and Pattaya, Thailand; Penang and Kuala Lumpur, Malaysia. Chart 22 was compiled by Forbes and The Huffington Post. They used 10 different variables and weighted them equally which resulted in the rankings:

Chart 22

Country	Buy or Rent	Benefits & Discounts	Visas & Residence	Cost of Living	Fitting In	Entert'mt & Amenities	Health Care	Healthy Lifestyle	Infrastructure	Climate	FINAL SCORES
Panama	86	100	100	89	97	100	89	95	90	89	93.5
Ecuador	100	99	83	90	92	95	85	95	85	100	92.4
Mexico	89	88	90	88	91	96	87	86	90	88	89.3
Costa Rica	88	79	87	86	95	88	92	98	88	83	88.4
Malaysia	94	67	87	90	95	100	94	90	87	74	87.8
Colombia	88	65	80	92	89	94	94	95	90	90	87.7
Thailand	90	72	70	90	90	96	88	80	89	83	84.8
Nicaragua	96	72	77	98	88	84	80	97	70	80	84.2
Spain	82	69	77	82	81	90	86	88	93	88	83.6
Portugal	82	75	77	85	81	81	81	88	93	86	82.9
Malta	80	75	78	83	94	82	83	75	93	85	82.8
Honduras	77	72	87	78	100	76	79	75	87	82	81.3
France	63	75	77	57	88	96	88	80	93	83	80.0
Belize	74	83	80	78	98	70	83	85	67	78	79.6
Peru	87	57	75	95	85	74	84	72	80	85	79.4
Italy	62	70	70	74	82	90	80	85	92	83	78.8
Philippines	63	75	67	85	92	90	88	67	89	69	78.5
Uruguay	67	63	67	65	90	98	88	73	90	83	78.4
Dom. Rep.	92	72	63	85	88	78	80	77	80	67	78.2
Ireland	80	75	77	65	98	84	72	72	93	65	78.1
Cambodia	76	57	80	100	83	89	75	83	63	74	78.0
Guatemala	82	63	77	91	75	78	75	70	76	85	77.2
Vietnam	70	63	60	90	65	58	74	72	57	76	68.5

In my opinion this ranking system is slightly flawed since some of the factors such as health care, climate and cost of living should be weighted more than other factors. Other relevant data that must be considered which were not included in the ranking system are the crime rate, safety and security, political stability of the countries and strength of their currencies. Climate, health care and taxes are certainly important for retirees, but any sudden policy and political changes by the host nation will have a severe effect on the retiree. It is hard enough trying to figure out the judicial system of the U.S., but you will be completely helpless in the Courts of Mexico, Nicaragua and Colombia if any legal issues come up for any reason. You will be at the mercy of local lawyers whose languages you may not even understand. You practically will no longer be under the protection of the United States. Another point for consideration, most of these nations will require you to directly deposit your social security and retirement income into a local bank. If the account is not a U.S. Dollar account, the exchange rates may fluctuate wildly and you may lose money due to policy and political changes and currency devaluations. For many retirees, the risks far outweigh the benefits.

- **Moving into a resort hotel**

The elderly joke about moving into a Holiday Inn when you retire is not a joke after all. The anonymous writer of the joke wrote, ***"With the average cost for a nursing home reaching $188 per day, there is a better way when we get old and feeble. I have already checked on reservations at the Holiday Inn. For a combined long-term stay discount and senior discount, it's $49.23 per night. That leaves $138.77 a day for breakfast, lunch, dinner in any restaurant I want, or room service. It also will leave enough for laundry, gratuities, and special TV movies. Plus, I'll get a swimming pool, a workout room, a lounge, and washer and dryer. I'll also get free toothpaste, razors, shampoo and soap. And I'll be treated like a customer, not a patient."***

But take note of this blog from a certain retiree by the name of Janet Beaudet who is writing about her real life experience: ***"Our room included TV, electricity, telephone, towels, bedding, desk, WIFI, furniture etc. The hotel was located in a parking lot with 7 restaurants, Pharmacy, medical facilities on the bus stop. A brook with picnic tables was across the street and we spent time feeding the ducks, etc. We had a kitchenette and made simple meals when we did not eat out. The grocery store was in walking distance but they delivered the groceries to our room and helped put them away. It was like living in paradise. If we did not have 4 children and 11 grandchildren at home we would have sold our house and stayed there***

indefinitely. I pay $6464.00 a month for 2 room suite including meals, some help getting dressed, occasional bed checks. I have to provide all my own furniture, linens, telephone, TV. My opinion is that if you can find a great location with a negotiated long term rate in a facility that is approved for long term tenants (zoning laws do not allow it in all hotels) and do not require extensive help and are willing to tip generously a hotel can be much better than Assisted Living and Cheaper."

Many popular hotel chains are now offering extended stay. It would not take much effort to shop around for the best deal for a year-long stay in the most ideal location you can find. These are some of the hotel chains that offer extended stay plans: Marriott, Mainstay Suites, Hilton, Hampton Inn, TownPlace Suites, Homewood Suites, Candlewood Suites and many others. Many of them advertise full kitchen and free Wi-Fi, free hot breakfast and evening social hours, health club, pool, lobby and outdoor space designed for socializing and free grocery delivery. When your year is up, you may want to move to a different exotic location or negotiate a renewal.

- **Cruise Ship Retirement**

This is yet again another rumor that has been making the rounds for years, i.e. a cruise ship retirement is cheaper than the cost of a nursing home. It turns out this happens more than you think but here is what my research reveals: The cost of an independent living facility is less than the cost of a cruise. The cost of an assisted living facility is more than the cost of a cruise. And the cost of a nursing home where you need level 3 care, i.e. assistance for activities of daily living (ADLs) and 24 hour on demand nursing care will cost a lot more than the cruise. Furthermore, a cruise ship will not be able to provide assistance for ADL and level 3 care. Due to our aging population, many of the popular cruise lines are now seriously discussing how to provide long term care on cruise ships. Their ships will have to be retrofitted to make them suitable for long term assisted living. For more information google: "Health care at sea".

Annuities, what are they?

Car leases and annuities are the most mysterious deals most people will ever encounter. In my experience with both products, the salesperson employs diversionary tactics and mumbo jumbo to convince you that you are getting a good deal. He will avoid telling you the equivalent effective annual interest rate you will be paying in case of an auto lease or that you will be receiving in case of an annuity. Instead, the salesperson will divert your attention towards the monthly payments you will be paying or receiving and other benefits and advantages these product may have over others. Annuity salesmen will neatly hide the deficiencies of these products within the very fine print of the contract that you will need a lawyer to review it and to tell you that what you are getting is a bad deal. That is the reason I have included this chapter in this book.

Think of annuities as "reverse-insurance". With an insurance policy, the sooner you die, the better it is financially speaking for your beneficiaries. You will pay less in premiums and your beneficiaries will immediately receive the tax-free death benefit. With an annuity, you either give the insurance company a lump sum or fund the annuity account with regular payments for a promise of a guaranteed income for a definite period of time or for as long as you live. The longer you live, the more money the insurance company will pay out. Some annuity contracts have long term care clauses and some of them have death benefit options.

I have concluded that annuities are not for me. I am looking for growth of my investments and I am willing to take the risk following my own system of saving and investing for a high return. But for people who are looking for preservation of capital, not growth, guaranteed return and do not mind turning over a big portion of their lifetime savings in one lump sum to an insurance company or fund an annuity contract (accumulation phase) for a period of time in return for a promise of principal protection, guaranteed income and perhaps to take care of the cost of long term care, annuities may be for you. The following information came from the U.S. Securities and Exchange Commission:

An annuity is a contract between you and an insurance company that requires the insurer to make payments to you, either immediately or in the future. You buy an annuity by making either a single payment or a series of payments. Similarly, your payout may come either as one lump-sum payment or as a series of payments over time.

People typically buy annuities to help manage their income in retirement. Annuities provide three things:

- Periodic payments for a specific amount of time. This may be for the rest of your life, or the life of your spouse or another person.
- Death benefits. If you die before receiving payments, the person you name as your beneficiary receives a specific payment.
- Tax-deferred growth. You pay no taxes on the income and investment gains from your annuity until you withdraw the money.

There are three basic types of annuities, fixed, variable and indexed. Here is how they work:

- Fixed annuity. The insurance company promises you a minimum rate of interest and a fixed amount of periodic payments. Fixed annuities are regulated by state insurance commissioners. Please check with your state insurance commission about the risks and benefits of fixed annuities and to confirm that your insurance broker is registered to sell insurance in your state.
- Variable annuity. The insurance company allows you to direct your annuity payments to different investment options, usually mutual funds. Your payout will vary depending on how much you put in, the rate of return on your investments, and expenses. The SEC regulates variable annuities.
- Indexed annuity. This annuity combines features of securities and insurance products. The insurance company credits you with a return that is based on a stock market index, such as the Standard & Poor's 500 Index. Indexed annuities are regulated by the state insurance commissioners.

Some people look to annuities to "insure" their retirement and to receive periodic payments once they no longer receive a salary. There are two phases to annuities, the accumulation phase and the payout phase.

- During the accumulation phase, you make payments that may be split among various investment options. In addition, variable annuities often allow you to put some of your money in an account that pays a fixed rate of interest.
- During the payout phase, you get your payments back, along with any investment income and gains. You may take the payout in one lump-sum payment, or you may choose to receive a regular stream of payments, generally monthly.

All investments carry a level of risk. Make sure you consider the financial strength of the insurance company issuing the annuity. You want to be sure the company will still be around, and financially sound, during your payout phase.

Variable annuities have a number of features that you need to understand before you invest. Understand that variable annuities are designed as an investment for long-term goals, such as retirement. They are not suitable for short-term goals because you typically will pay substantial taxes and charges or other penalties if you withdraw your money early. Variable annuities also involve investment risks, just as mutual funds do.

Insurance companies sell annuities, as do some banks, brokerage firms, and mutual fund companies. Make sure you read and understand your annuity contract. All fees should be clearly stated in the contract. Your most important source of information about investment options within a variable annuity is the mutual fund prospectus. Request prospectuses for all the mutual fund options you might want to select. Read the prospectuses carefully before you decide how to allocate your purchase payments among the investment options.

Realize that if you are investing in a variable annuity through a tax-advantaged retirement plan, such as a 401(k) plan or an Individual Retirement Account, you will get no additional tax advantages from a variable annuity. In such cases, consider buying a variable annuity only if it makes sense because of the annuity's other features.

Note that if you sell or withdraw money from a variable annuity too soon after your purchase, the insurance company will impose a "surrender charge." This is a type of sales charge that applies in the "surrender period," typically six to eight years after you buy the annuity. Surrender charges will reduce the value of -- and the return on -- your investment.

You will pay several charges when you invest in a variable annuity. Be sure you understand all charges before you invest. Besides surrender charges, there are a number of other charges, including:

- Mortality and expense risk charge. This charge is equal to a certain percentage of your account value, typically about 1.25% per year. This charge pays the issuer for the insurance risk it assumes under the annuity contract. The profit from this charge sometimes is used to pay a commission to the person who sold you the annuity.
- Administrative fees. The issuer may charge you for record keeping and other administrative expenses. This may be a flat annual fee, or a percentage of your account value.
- Underlying fund expenses. In addition to fees charged by the issuer, you will pay the fees and expenses for underlying mutual fund investments.
- Fees and charges for other features. Additional fees typically apply for special features, such as a guaranteed minimum income benefit or long-term care insurance. Initial sales loads, fees for transferring part of your account from one investment option to another, and other fees also may apply.
- Penalties. If you withdraw money from an annuity before you are age 59 ½, you may have to pay a 10% tax penalty to the Internal Revenue Service on top of any taxes you owe on the income.

Variable annuities are considered to be securities. All broker-dealers and investment advisers that sell variable annuities must be registered. Before buying an annuity from a broker or adviser, confirm that they are registered using BrokerCheck and click on this website, **FINRA's BrokerCheck website**.

In most cases, the investments offered within a variable annuity are mutual funds. By law, each mutual fund is required to file a prospectus and regular shareholder reports with the SEC. Before you invest, be sure to read these materials.

If the preceding article from the SEC does not yet discourage you on buying annuities, read on. Fixed and Indexed annuities are in essence insurance contracts. Most of them are sold by insurance companies such as Allstate, Fidelity Insurance, John Hancock, Met Life, AXA, Prudential and others. Variable annuities are in essence insured investments in mutual funds and are generally sold by brokerage firms. Annuities are not guaranteed by the government. Your money will disappear if the annuity provider disappears. The most common slogan of annuity salesmen is: "You make money when the stock market goes up, but you won't lose money when the stock market goes down". They insure the "annual percentage yield" on fixed and indexed annuities and you pay a premium for that guaranteed return. The annual expenses can be as much as 3% a year. Example, if an annuity is indexed to the S&P 500 which averaged 10% in one year, your annuity will earn a return of 7% that year. On the other hand, you are protected on the down side and your annuity will still earn a minimum return even in a year when the S&P 500 had a negative yield. I prefer my own investment and allocation of asset strategy.

Before signing a contract, make sure to read the fine print. Better still, in your first meeting with the broker, request a prospectus that you can take home with you. It is important to ask about principal protection (insurance), annual fees on fixed and variable, long term care rider, investment options, death benefits and annuity payout options.

If you still think that an annuity may be right for you, the website below is an excellent source for additional information for fixed annuities.

https://www.immediateannuities.com/information/annuity-rates-step-1.html

Enter the lump sum amount you want to annuitize today. Enter your age and other pertinent information. Various offers of monthly payouts will pop up for the amount you want to annuitize. If you click on the (?) the terms are explained in plain non-legalese language. The payout amounts shown represent interest and return of principal. After the page with your information pops up, you will notice that there are different pay outs and types of coverages such as "Joint Life", "Single Life" and "Period Certain" options, e.g. for life, 25, 20, 15, 10 and 5 years.

After I entered information for a person who just reached full retirement age (FRA) which at the time of writing is age 66, has $300,000 to invest and wants a monthly payout for a 10-year period certain, with no cost of living increase, I received a best offer of $2,780 monthly payment. This annuity payout represents a 2.18% annual percent return on the money. You may confirm the rate of return by clicking on the website below. Enter the initial principal amount = $300,000 and monthly withdrawal = $2780.00 annuitized over 10 years, then click calculate to see the annual growth rate.

http://www.bankrate.com/calculators/investing/annuity-calculator.aspx

My opinion is that I can do a lot better than a 2.18% APR by investing on my own.

The payouts include principal and interest, so the interest portion of the annuity is taxable as ordinary income. Click on this IRS website for information on how the interest is calculated, https://www.irs.gov/taxtopics/tc411.html

Retiring within 10 years

It is never too late to save for retirement if you have the resources. You should continue dumping as much money as you can afford into your retirement account. If I think I will need my money within 10 years, I will reduce volatility by moving the amount of money I think I would need into high quality short term and long term bond funds, AA or AAA rated only. I will stay away from the so-called high yield bond funds. They probably include lots of junk bonds in their portfolio. A bond fund should make more money than a money market fund.

If you are ten years away from retirement and have not saved at least $500,000, you must read, study and implement the budgeting strategy in the book, ***("DynBudgTech")*** to help you control your expenses and build wealth in the few remaining years of your working life. Suze Orman's op-ed stating that a retiree needs at least $3 million in savings to comfortably retire should scare you into taking control of your finances at this late stage of your life. Remember, you can still do it if you implement the suggestions in the aforementioned book.

Retiring within 5 years

If I am retiring within 5 years and think that I may need some of my principal within that time, I would get out of equities all together. The market may be against me when I need to take out some of the money. So I will divide the balance of my portfolio into several high quality bond funds (government, corporate and municipal) with ratings of AA and AAA only. Although there is less volatility in bond funds than equity funds, the bond fund values will still go down during the bear market that follows a recession. Perhaps not by 30% to 60% like stocks usually do but 20% to 30%. If I do not think I will need to take out any money at all within 5 years, i.e. I can leave my portfolio alone for 5 years, then I will invest the full amount as outlined under Chapter, "**Investing in Retirement**".

To avoid losing 20 to 30% of your money, it is still absolutely necessary to continue to follow the timing system in the book, ***"Path2Wealth".***

Other investments before and during retirement

100% in Bonds - If your risk tolerance is a lot lower than mine, i.e. if a 10% to 50% drop in the stock market will drive you crazy, then put your entire portfolio into 4 different bond funds that are rated AA+. Avoid a fund that has junk bonds in it. Select funds that have a "below average risk" rating. You will not receive a return of 13% to 20% APR during bull markets as you would in Small Caps or Emerging market equity funds, but in the long run, say 15 years, you will average just slightly lower. Best of all, you can put your money in and forget it.

For those of you who are about to retire, saved a substantial amount of money, say $2 million or more of cash and are hoping to live off the income from dividends and leave the principal to your heirs, check out high quality dividend paying stocks from solid companies with a record of profitability which are not likely to go out of business in this lifetime. Click on the website below for more information:

http://www.dividend.com/

For example, you can divide your $2 million equally into several quality dividend stocks such as Astra-Zeneca, Glaxo-Smith-Kline, Hanes Brands, Nike, Walt Disney, Apple, Microsoft, Intel Corp, Pepsi-Cola, Coca-Cola, Johnson & Johnson, 3M Company, Procter & Gamble, McDonald's, AT&T, General Electric, Anheuser-Busch, Nestle', Exxon-Mobile, Chevron, Phillips, Stanley Black & Decker, Deere and IBM.

The aforementioned companies are used as examples only and are not specifically recommended. Do your due diligence as to the financial strength and viability of each company.

Investing in retirement & required minimum distribution (RMD)

I am confident that I will reach my goal in retirement, of having a fully paid house and having enough money to last me well into my 90s if I live that long. When that retirement day comes, I will do a lot of fishing. I do not want to spend much time worrying how my retirement savings is doing today. I want my biggest worry to be figuring out how much money I should donate to charities this week, what kind of fish to catch today, how to cook my catch and what type of wine goes well with my catch. So as soon as I stop working, I will re-allocate my assets this way, 40% in a Large-Cap value fund, 40% in a Mid-Cap value fund, 20% in a short-term government Bond Fund. I will re-balance my portfolio each quarter. I will limit my withdrawals to 4% per annum or the RMD whichever is lower. I will take my withdrawals from the Bond Fund. I will continue to monitor the stock market according to my system explained in my book, ***"Path2Wealth"*** so I can get out of stocks before the next stock market crash and get back into the market before the start of the bull market that follows the crash.

Note that there is a strict rule on RMDs. Penalty is severe, a whopping 50% on the required undistributed amount. You must take the RMD by April 1 of the year following the year you turned 70 ½. Open these IRS links for more information,

https://www.irs.gov/pub/irs-tege/uniform_rmd_wksht.pdf

https://www.irs.gov/publications/p590b/ch01.html#en_US_2016_publink1000230772

https://www.irs.gov/retirement-plans/plan-participant-employee/required-minimum-distribution-worksheets

The IRS links above will take you to a worksheet to figure out your RMD. If you are still working at age 70 1/2, you don't have to take RMDs from your current employer's 401k plan until you leave your job. This is the "still working exception". To qualify for this exception, you must be considered employed throughout the entire year, own no more than 5% of the company and your 401k plan allows you to delay RMDs. For this reason, it is a good idea to transfer all of your other taxable retirement accounts, traditional 401k and IRAs to your current employer's plan if your plan accepts rollovers so as to avoid the annual RMD if you don't need to take any of the money out. However, if you are already 70 ½, you must first take the RMD from your IRA before rolling the balance over to you company's 401k plan.

RMD rules are complex and the rules often change. The explanations in the IRS website will confuse the average tax payer. A seasoned accountant, retirement planner or tax professional can simplify the rules and customize an RMD plan for you but here is the general idea behind the RMD rules. If your spouse is the sole beneficiary of your IRA or 401k, he or she will inherit your plan and the same rules will apply as if it's his or hers. For unmarried owners of the plan and married owners whose spouses are not more than 10 years younger, and owners whose spouses are not the sole beneficiaries of their plan, the following distribution table:

Chart 23

Unmarried Owners, Married Owners whose Spouses are not more than 10 Years younger, and married owners whose spouses are not the sole beneficiaries of their IRAs

Age	Distribution Period	Age	Distribution Period
70	27.4	93	9.6
71	26.5	94	9.1
72	25.6	95	8.6
73	24.7	96	8.1
74	23.8	97	7.6
75	22.9	98	7.1
76	22	99	6.7
77	21.2	100	6.3
78	20.3	101	5.9
79	19.5	102	5.5
80	18.7	103	5.2
81	17.9	104	4.9
82	17.1	105	4.5
83	16.3	106	4.2
84	15.5	107	3.9
85	14.8	108	3.7
86	14.1	109	3.4
87	13.4	110	3.1
88	12.7	111	2.9
89	12	112	2.6
90	11.4	113	2.4
91	10.8	114	2.1
92	10.2	115 and over	1.9

According to the table 23, if you were 70 ½ years old by the end of the year, and your plan balance is $1,000,000 your RMD is $36,496.35 (balance divided by life expectancy). You must take this distribution by April 1 of the following year but you should take it before year end so you won't get stuck with 2 RMDs the following year which may put you in a higher tax bracket.

The rules are more complicated for plan owners whose spouses are more than 10 years younger and are the sole beneficiaries of their spouse's plan. In the wisdom of our legislators who have hundreds of actuaries, tax experts and economists working for them all day long, they came up with a system for RMD based on "Joint Life and Last Survivor Expectancy". They devised RMD Table II (Table) to come up with a "blended" life expectancy for the owner and survivor. The rationale behind this is that the government does not want to wait too long to collect taxes on the older spouse's plan. The website below is an excellent resource for figuring out your RMD. Just enter the required information and click "calculate". A report will show up on the screen and you can print a PDF report of the table.

https://www.calcxml.com/calculators/qua07;jsessionid=F658D4F9462B62CA072EAEC8D35DDDCE?skn=#

If you have retired and are one of the lucky top 10% who have more than a million dollars in your retirement accounts, take at least the annual RMD and pay the taxes. You should not outlive your money if it is invested the way I have outlined in the beginning of this chapter and if you do not lose the typical 30 to 60% drop in assets whenever the market crashes.

If you need more money, take more than the RMD. If your money earns at least 4% APR you will be taking out approximately $40,000 to $65,000 a year until you are over 100 years old. Pay the tax each year. It would not be so bad. Don't be too greedy. You have successfully used the tax system to your advantage, why not pay your due now? Most people have less income in retirement than when they were working. If you're the opposite, be glad, thank God and pay the taxes. Follow the taxation advice in PART II and PART III. If you maximize your deferral and take advantage of all the legal tax deductions, you will have paid much less in taxes by the time you retire than others who will not follow my advice. Some financial advisors recommend buying a QLAC (Qualified Longevity Annuity Contract) at this point to defer RMD and tax payment, but I would not recommend them. Take the RMD and pay the taxes annually now at this point in your life rather than defer the taxes until you are 85 years old. If you have dependents depending on you for financial support, pay some of their expenses from the after-tax money. Check with your tax accountant if you may be able to claim any of them as dependents (qualifying relatives) on your tax return so as to reduce your taxes. Better still, if you have too much money, give some of your RMD to your favorite charity via Qualified Charitable Distribution (QCD) to reduce your taxes. The distribution will not count as income and it is easy to set up but it must be done correctly. So check with your tax accountant on how to accomplish this. Another option is to just take the RMD and reinvest the after tax money following the strategy in this book. Some financial advisors recommend buying a life insurance policy with the RMD if you don't need any of the money to live on. That way you can leave tax free money (insurance death benefit proceeds) to your beneficiaries. But is this really more advantageous than just leaving taxable inheritance to your heirs? Review the charts in Part IV, "Insurance Policy vs. IRA" and decide for yourself. If you are adamant about minimizing taxes in retirement, another option that many finance gurus (aka "Financial Entertainers") advocate is to start a foundation so as to reduce your taxes. Click on the link below to learn more:

http://www.thebusinessofgood.org/get-engaged/starting-a-foundation.aspx

According to these finance gurus you may be able to deduct many business expenses (*wink wink*) from your tax returns if you have a foundation. Examples of these "business expenses" are: vacations, cruises, casino trips, cars, yachts, gardening, janitorial services and many other expenses that may be connected with your foundation. In a recent guest appearance on WOR radio, a NYC based station, a popular radio talk show host of the 1990s said you can use your yacht or go on a cruise and deduct the expenses from your taxes if your trips were related to your charitable work. He gave examples such as, attending a party in Paris, investigating wildlife in the Galapagos or touring Costa Rica to observe the bird population in the wilderness so you can decide if it is worth it to donate money to the Audubon Society. He concluded by saying, "The IRS does not like it but there is nothing they can do until Congress changes the tax system. You are not breaking the law". As for me, do I really want to get involved in any of this in my old age? If I have 2 million dollars at the age of 70, with my lifestyle, I will never spend it all in my lifetime. And how much money to leave my children is really not that important to me nor to them. So in retirement, all I want to plan for today, tomorrow and the following day is, "where am I going fishing?" I also want to plan a trip every couple of months to every exotic location in the world I can think of. Right now I am thinking of Bora Bora, Bhutan, Myanmar, Galapagos, Maldives, Alice Springs, Victoria Falls, Machu Picchu, Cape Town and hundreds of other tourist spots on my bucket list. Geeeeeez, I can't wait!

Where to Invest Your Excess RMD

If you follow the retirement strategy in this book and the investment strategy in the ***"Path2Wealth"***, you should have excess RMD that you will not need to live on. How should you invest this extra money? Many financial advisors are so focused on avoiding taxes that they put their clients' portfolios into tax free vehicles such as whole life insurance, tax exempt municipal bonds, dividend paying stocks that qualify for capital gains tax rates, energy partnerships, foreign stocks and Treasury bonds. The problem with this strategy is that these low tax and tax free investments will yield 2% to 3.5% APY whereas my portfolio will yield 10% to 12% average APY. Even if the earnings are taxed as earned income and 85% of my SS benefits are taxed, my calculation shows that I still come out ahead following my investment strategy. Do the math and see what is more beneficial for you---to earn 10% to 12% APY and pay the tax or earn 2% to 3.5% APY on your money and pay very little tax. The numbers may surprise you.

Enrich Your Life by Exploring the World

Travel used to be unaffordable. Many Americans waited till retirement when they felt they had enough money to explore the world. Unfortunately, by retirement age most people are not fit enough to climb up and down tour buses, let alone walk to tourist attractions to take pictures. Whenever I join sightseeing tours, I always feel sorry for senior citizens who beg the tour guides to let them remain on the bus on stop-overs requiring a short walk to a certain tourist spot.

Why wait until retirement to explore the world? Why not do it now and enrich your life and the lives of your children? After all, if you follow the wealth building advice in this book you are destined to have enough money to last your lifetime. Take two meaningful trips every year. Explore the national parks for at least two weeks in summer and go overseas for at least a week between November and New Year's Day. Most companies offer a 2-week paid vacation each year, and many companies offer 3 weeks after a certain period of employment. Most companies in Western Europe offer at least one month vacation every year. Travel is easier than you think. Nowadays, you do not need a travel agent. You yourself, on your own, can book your flights, car rentals and hotels online through travel websites such as Travelocity, Orbitz, PriceLine, Kayak, Expedia, TravelAdvisor.com, Hotel.com and Bookings.com. For local sightseeing tours, I like Grayline and Viator. You can snag some "real bargains" from any of the above-mentioned websites, e.g. $125 a night at Elbow Beach Hotel in Bermuda in the month of May and accommodations at four star hotels for about $100 per night during the low season in Rome, Paris, London, Munich, Amsterdam and Geneva. Because I have been following my own advice, I have visited most of America's 58 National Parks. My favorites are Arches, Canyonlands, Bryce Canyon, Glacier Bay, Zion, Grand Canyons, Yellowstone, Shenandoah, Acadia, Sequoia and Volcanoes National Park. I love driving so I do not mind driving thousands of miles while enjoying the scenery on the way to a certain destination. Some of the most scenic routes I've driven on America's highways are from Hilo to Kona in the big island of Hawaii; Highway 1 from Half Moon Bay to Santa Cruz; Highway 5 Sacramento to Vancouver, Canada; Highway 70 Denver to Provo, UT; Highway 191 Crescent Junction to Bluff, UT; Highway 89A from Lake Powell to Kanab; Lolo Pass Road from Mt. Hood Highway 26 to Lost Lake, Oregon;

Highway 75 from Sault St. Marie to Mackinaw City; Skyline Drive, Shenandoah National Park; NYC to Montreal via Taconic Parkway; Highway 81 from Scranton to Syracuse. Whenever time permits, I find a way to rent a car to take in the scenery and explore the countryside even in foreign countries. The most memorable road trips I've taken were from Puerto Vallarta to Guadalajara; London to Bristol; Chamonix to Pisa; Salzburg to Venice; Torino to Rome and Berlin to Luxembourg. I estimate that I have spent over $200,000 in travel expenses in the past 20 years. For me, this is money well spent. Travel has been good for my family and me, for our health and well-being. My children had travelled to several foreign destinations before starting high school. The priceless experiences opened their eyes on how other people outside America live, on what side of the road they drive, the languages they speak and the food they eat. Most importantly, I've opened my children's eyes on how lucky and privileged they are to be living in America. I was born with wanderlust. As soon as I complete one journey, I am planning and looking forward to the next one. That is why I just don't understand people who have not yet caught this "disease". I have a friend who can well afford to travel but who says he does not want to go to Hawaii because "it's too far". There are those who fly to exotic places then sit by the pool reading a book and sipping margaritas all day long. I have a friend who goes to Cape Cod in the summer and flies to Las Vegas in November, year after year.

Whenever I travel to a new place, I like exploring the food, talking to the locals even in sign language and going to the market places where they go. I can only hope that you readers will catch wanderlust and find yourselves booking trips to wonderful destinations such as Bhutan; Seychelles; Maldives; Goa, India; Machu Picchu, Peru; Kathmandu, Nepal; Durban, South Africa; Alice Springs, Australia; Petra, Jordan; Masada National Park, Israel; Chamonix, France; Interlaken, Switzerland; Naples, Italy. Before you leave this world, don't you want to see the land of the midnight sun, the Alps, Pompeii, Stonehenge, the Eiffel Tower, the Great Wall of China, Taj Mahal and a phenomenon called Aurora Borealis? For just once in your life don't you want to experience an overnight stay at one of those ice hotels in Finland? Think of the money you will spend as a small investment for your mind and spirit. Many years from now if you end up in a nursing home and cannot walk anymore, you might still remember those amazing trips that you took in your youth and tell stories of your wonderful experiences to anyone who would be kind enough to listen.

Staying Healthy and Fit as You Age

I must preface this chapter by warning the reader that this is not an attempt to give medical advice. I included this chapter to relate my own personal story for entertainment purpose only or for whatever benefit it may give the reader. Do not act on any information in this book without consulting your doctor.

If a doctor goes by my family health history it would be easy for him to conclude that I only have a short life to live. My paternal grandfather and ALL my paternal granduncles died of either heart disease, heart attacks or strokes. Many died in their forties and fifties. My paternal grandmother and most of my paternal grand aunts died of diabetes also at a relatively young age, in their fifties and early sixties. My father's side of the family was always plagued with elevated triglyceride, high cholesterol levels and high blood pressure. My mother's side of the family was plagued with asthma, emphysema and chronic pulmonary diseases. None of my grandparents, grand uncles and grand aunts died of old age.

Due to my family history and my own ignorance, in my first 30 years of life my diet consisted of low fat, low protein and high carbohydrates. For breakfast I ate bread, pancakes, donuts, muffins, cereals, waffles, bagels and cakes. I avoided eggs (because they have high cholesterol content), bacon, sausages, butter, cheese, ham and steaks. For lunch I loaded up on pasta, bread, rice, French fries and all types of starches you can imagine. My dinner consisted mostly of different types of starches and vegetables with very little meat (because they are high on cholesterol). My annual check-up just a few days shy of my 30th birthday revealed that I had hypoglycemia and my doctor recommended that I change my diet. I must have misunderstood him because the way I changed my diet was to add on more meat to my diet without easing off on my sugar and starch intake. The result was disastrous. I gradually gained weight and the result of my blood test a year later confirmed that whatever I was doing was not working. I had elevated cholesterol and triglyceride levels, my glucose was high and my blood pressure was consistently 160/90. It was only then that it became clear to me that my doctor's advice was for me to reduce carbohydrate intake---not necessarily to increase protein. It was extremely difficult to heed my doctor's advice. I am the type of person who can consume a half gallon container of Breyers vanilla ice cream in one sitting.

Oftentimes, I even added vodka or brandy to it. But just the same, chances are if I opened a half gallon container, it did not make it back to the freezer.

My day of reckoning came in the mid-90s when I went to San Francisco for a 2 day conference. My flight was scheduled to depart at 3pm from Newark airport. I worked for a tour operator so I often travelled first class for free. I planned to forgo lunch to take full advantage of the perks, i.e. the in-flight first class meal and free adult beverages. I had a big corn muffin at my desk about 8 that morning and around 10am, someone brought out a big cake on the occasion of an office mate's birthday so I took a big piece of it. I was hungry when I got to the airport at 2pm but I said to myself "I can bear it" for another half hour until boarding time. I don't know how it is now since I have not been in first class for quite some time but back then, the airline crew pampered first class passengers and served them alcoholic drinks as soon as they were seated. We had priority boarding and by the time the last passenger boarded, I had already consumed 2 glasses of champagne. Before the plane moved I finished three more drinks, 3 shots of Chivas and gobbled up an assortment of appetizers. Then the flight attendants cleaned up and folded back our tray tables. As the plane was taking off, I felt a little nauseous and could not wait until the "fasten your seat belt sign" was turned off. I had a window seat and the seat next to mine was vacant so I was able to quickly get up and run towards the lavatory. The next thing I remember I am lying on the aisle and I am hearing a woman's voice on the PA announcing "if there is a doctor on the plane please come over..." I soon realized I passed out on my way to the lavatory. A stewardess has loosened my belt, unbuttoned my pants and held me down when I tried to get up, saying "stay on your back sir, the doctor is coming". Soon the doctor was examining me while I was lying on the floor and asking me questions. "Do you have any medical conditions? Why do you think you passed out?" By then I've regained my senses so I calmly replied, "I have hypoglycemia and I think I had too much to drink with too little to eat". "You should take a return flight as soon as this plane lands. You need a full examination", he suggested. The stewardess helped me get up and got me back to me seat. "Do you have pain in your chest?" she asked, pointing to her own chest. "No, why? And where are my glasses?" I inquired with a puzzled look on my face. "They're in your shirt pocket, you took a really hard fall". I took my eye glasses out of my pocket. They were bent out of shape and I had to twist them back into shape so I could wear them. I felt better two hours into the flight after eating the first class meal the airline served. I refrained from any alcoholic drinks and only ordered diet coke, tea and coffee. I felt soreness in my chest area so I went to the lavatory to check it out. When I unbuttoned my shirt I noticed a 2 inch by 2 inch welt in the middle of my chest. I also noticed a bruise on my forehead just above my right eye. The locations of the injuries led me to believe that when I lost consciousness, I must have fallen forward, face first then bumped my forehead on the back of an empty seat then my chest must have hit the armrest. I learned two important lessons from this eye opening experience. First, when you become unconscious you will feel no pain. There must be something in our brain that disconnects the pain receptors. A protective mechanism that protects us from pain. Second, I was not healthy.

So when I got back home, I immediately called my PCP and related my experience on the plane. He ordered different types of tests for me which were done over the course of 2 months. These included blood work, electrocardiogram, nuclear stress test and glucose tolerance test. His diagnosis is that I was pre-diabetic and I had hypertension and elevated cholesterol. So, at the age of 32, my doctor put me on Lipitor to lower my cholesterol and a beta blocker for hypertension. And he threatened to put me on diabetes medication if I fail to shape up. To make a long story short, I struggled for 7 years, gradually gaining weight, experiencing palpitations, extreme fatigue, drowsiness at around 3pm, insomnia and sleep apnea. I am only 5'8" and ballooned to almost 200 Lbs. If I walked only a few blocks or climbed the stairs I had trouble catching my breath. My life changed when my son who was then in high school asked me, "Dad, why don't you walk around the yard instead of spending the entire day in front of the television?" The rhetorical question hit me like a lightning bolt. The next day, I walked around the yard for 15 minutes just to show my son that his dad is not a lazy bum. Then each day, though I struggled, I picked myself up and walked a few more steps until I started jogging, then running a mile, then 2 miles a day. I got my old bike repaired and biked for long periods on weekends, sometimes for 4 hours almost non-stop. Although I lost 10 pounds quickly due to the physical activity, I was not able to take control of my diet until I accidentally came across a book entitled "Protein Power" by Drs. Michael and Mary Eades. Two statements in the book became etched in my mind, "The body does not need carbohydrates..." and, "...fats in the absence of carbohydrates are good..." (Paraphrased). Since I secretly love fats anyway, I resolved to give the diet a try. I followed the high protein diet by eating 2 eggs and bacon for breakfast, broccoli and fried chicken or a burger with no bun for lunch and chicken, fish, pork chop or steak and leafy green vegetables for dinner. It was terrible at first! I badly craved for some bread, pasta, potatoes, rice and sweets. But after only 15 days on this "protein power diet", what a surprise! I lost 15 pounds! The best part is that my blood work taken 1 month after I began this diet showed my cholesterol, triglycerides and glucose all went down to normal levels. My blood pressure was consistently much lower than normal for 3 months so my doctor took me off the hypertension medication. I continued taking only the Lipitor.

That was 15 years ago. I have an occasional craving for sweets and starches and on those occasions, I make an exception and still consume a half gallon container of Breyers vanilla ice cream in one sitting just to get it out of my system. But generally, I remained faithful to the diet and I try to limit my carbohydrate intake to 35 grams a day. I feel much stronger today, physically and mentally than 20 years ago. My weight is down to 165. I kept up with walking, jogging and running at least half an hour every day. In fact, I stopped taking Lipitor 2 years ago but did not tell my doctor. Thank God my blood test readings are still all normal even without taking any regular medications. My doctor keeps telling me, "Continue doing whatever you're doing....", so I continue eating eggs, bacon and steaks. I have so much energy that I now go to the gym thrice a week for strengthening and conditioning.

In summary, I eat a low carb diet, exercise at least half an hour each day, I almost always drink 2 glasses of wine with dinner, I drink at least 8 glasses of water every day, I usually get 7 to 8 hours of sleep and I go out of my way to avoid any type of stress. Stress can cause anxiety and depression and can weaken the immune system. When I'm feeling stressed out and I feel that my mind is in turmoil, I do the following:

- While sitting in front of my desk, I put my elbows on my desk, my hands on my face, empty my mind so I am thinking of nothing, which is similar to what others may refer to as meditation, hold my breath, try to tense all the muscles in my body from head to toe, then exhale. I repeat the process 3 or 4 times.

- Then I push my chair back, grasp the front of my desk and do 15 squats, as shown on the following picture. I do at least 3 sets of this exercise every day. Squat exercises offer many types of benefits. Click on this link to find out more: http://www.beautyandtips.com/sports-and-fitness/10-benefits-of-squats-and-why-every-girl-should-try-doing-squat-exercises/

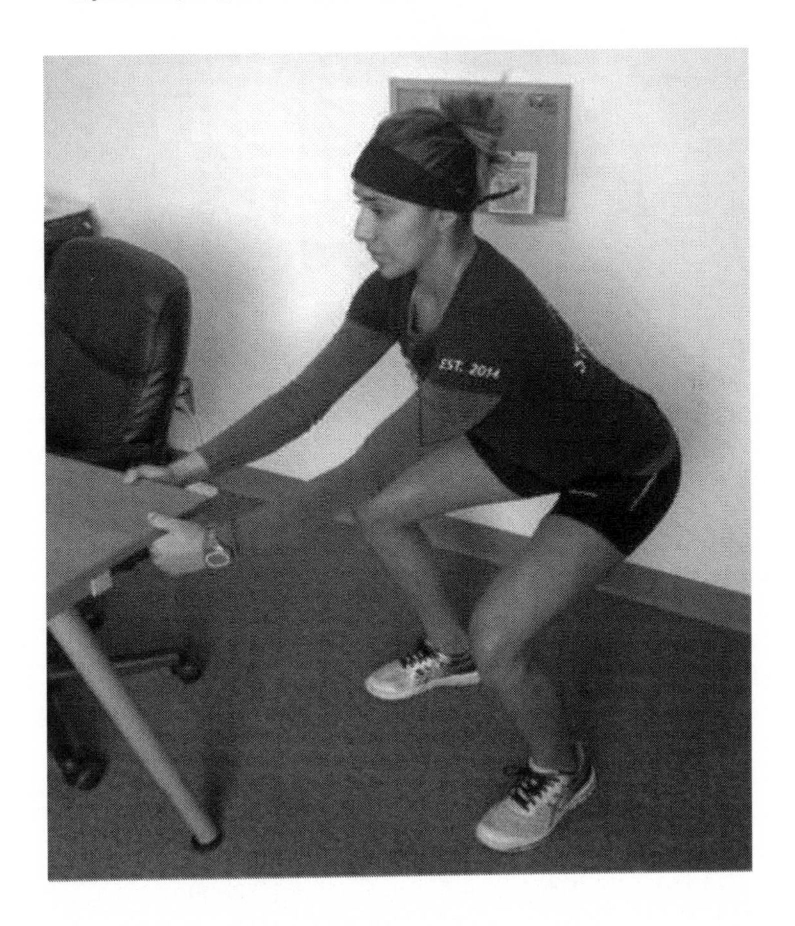

- If I am home, I do plank exercises or push-ups and sit-ups, doing as many repetitions as I can.

How does the new tax law affect the retirement strategies in this book?

The passage of The tax reform bill into law, now officially known as the Tax Cuts and Jobs Act of 2017 ("TCJA") Public law no. 115-97, only proves my point that we should NOT focus too much on taxes when formulating an investment and retirement strategy. Making long term investment and retirement plans based on taxation is an exercise in futility because future tax rates and other tax changes are unknowable. The pendulum swings the other way every 8 years. The tax cuts in this recently passed TCJA will expire in 2025. If a Democrat wins back the White House and the Democrats take back the House and Senate, it is almost certain the Trump Tax Cuts will be allowed to expire and the tax rates will revert back to the 2017 tax brackets. Moreover, tax increases are likely when Democrats are back in power. That's not a political statement. It's just a fact of life.

There are so many variables in your own personal savings and investment situation and idiosyncrasies in the way you manage your life that I am sure you don't really know how the new tax law will affect you. For this reason, I've decided to publish a new book entitled:

How Much Federal Income Tax Will I Pay in 2018?

https://www.amazon.com/Much-Federal-Income-Will-2018-ebook/dp/B078Z5LXGJ/ref=sr_1_1/146-7233552-6714568?s=digital-text&ie=UTF8&qid=1516034997&sr=1-1&keywords=Arthur V. Prosper

The book contains comparison charts of how much federal tax you will pay under the current tax system and how much you will pay under the new system. All you have to do is choose the table that closely resembles your income level, filing status and deductions. If none of the charts is applicable to your own unique situation, email **Arthur V. Prosper** for the editable excel tax worksheet. Copy and paste the Program Code below. When you receive the excel worksheet, you can enter your income level and deductions on the spreadsheet. The taxes for 2017 and 2018 will automatically calculate.

Email address: Arthur V. Prosper@Arthur V. Prosper.com

Copy and Paste: **Editable Excel Worksheet Program Code: SMD0821**

Conclusion

A healthy and stress-free lifestyle is the best gift you can give to yourself and to your loved ones. What is the point of living longer in retirement if you are in poor health, living in constant pain and you have become a burden to your family?

The retirement strategy in this book is a straight-line route towards a six million dollar retirement nest egg. Sufficient retirement savings will minimize your stress, worries and anxieties. Enough money will improve your quality of life in retirement. When you have this amount of money in retirement, you can eschew any of the other investments and retirement schemes financial and retirement planners, insurance agents and annuity salesmen try to sell you. Annuities, permanent life insurance, tax free retirement planning, Medicaid planning, Elder care planning, ILIT, long term care planning, QLAC, Dynasty Trust, J&S Insurance Policy, Family Bank RMD, family foundations, off-shore accounts and other products may not benefit you at all (see the Chapter, **INSURANCE POLICY vs. IRA**). Do the math like I did in the various charts shown in this book to make sure you understand what you are getting into. The sellers of these products won't even be able to explain them to you in language that you can understand. You will pay them their expensive professional fee and they may not be around in 20 years when you need them. In many cases, what you think you bought is not what they sold you. Many of these insurance products are riddled with fine prints that you will need a lawyer to explain the plans to you and after doing the math you may realize that you would be better off to leave your retirement savings alone, take the RMD, pay the taxes and reinvest the after tax proceeds that you don't need to live on. Your calculation may show, as mine did, that you will leave your heirs more money by following the strategy in this book. I believe "Retirement Planning" is a whole new industry that was created that only a select few actually benefit from. If insurance companies lose money by selling permanent life insurance and annuities, they will ALL be out of business. Follow the steps shown in this book. You and your spouse will have $6 million dollars when you reach full retirement age and you will leave more money to your heirs. What can be simpler than saving $1000 dollars a month inside your retirement account, investing the money wisely so that you will not lose a penny of it, earning 10% annual return, buying your principal residence and collecting SS benefits at the right time? It is time to implement this stress-free game plan while you are still young. When you stop worrying, you start enjoying, you start living. Life is good. Make it even better in retirement!

****

If this book helped you, your positive Amazon Review would be much appreciated.

****

If you have questions or comments, VISIT THE AUTHOR'S WEBSITE and click "Ask Arthur V. Prosper":

http://Arthur V. Prosper.com/contact/

http://Arthur V. Prosper.com/

Living Rich & Loving It
Learn more about the following subjects from the author's new book, Living Rich & Loving It

https://www.amazon.com/Living-Rich-Loving-healthy-balanced-ebook/dp/B01GORIB4Y/ref=sr_1_3?s=digital-text&ie=UTF8&qid=1471625403&sr=1-3&keywords=Arthur V. Prosper

- **Find a job you love – If you cannot wait to get up and get to work every morning, then you have found the job you love. Otherwise, you need to read this chapter and the chapter, "Increase Your Income with these Ideas".**

- **Personal Insurance – Which is better, whole life or term insurance? How much insurance do you need? The answer may surprise you.**

- **Planning for College – how to fund your children's college education. Read the many different ideas in this chapter which includes the availability of financial aid packages. The chart shows which colleges to choose and guides you towards a prudent decision.**

- **Increase Your Income - Make more money in your spare time with these ideas. When you read the money-making ideas in this chapter, you will scratch your head and say, "why didn't I think of that?"**

- **Create a Document Storage and Retrieval System – So simple yet so effective. It will free up a lot of your limited living space.**

- **Stress-Free Personal Time Management – This system will organize your day and free up plenty of your time for use at your leisure.**

- **How to Store and Safeguard Passwords – Simple trick will help you create and remember strong passwords.**

- **Learn more, click on the link below:**
  https://www.amazon.com/Living-Rich-Loving-healthy-balanced-ebook/dp/B01GORIB4Y/ref=pd_sim_sbs_351_2?ie=UTF8&psc=1&refRID=825N2SZCEYGWC1STH495

****

Excerpt from the book, Living Rich & Loving It:
LIVE A RICH, HAPPY, HEALTHY, SIMPLE AND BALANCED LIFE

Life does not have to be complicated. If you succeed in following the life strategies in this book, your children will end up well, your investments will provide you with a nice retirement nest egg that will last for as long as you live, you will minimize stress in your life and you will have more time for leisure and for activities that help keep your mind and body healthy. This book is not the magic bullet for success but a playbook to improve your odds for achieving success. There will be unexpected twists and turns in your life but the principles and strategies in this book will help lead you to the correct path to success and keep you on track to achieve all you want in life. If you have goals, dreams and aspirations in life, you have a sense of direction but you still need a road map to take you from here to there. I hope this book will serve as that road map for you.

Having a balanced life for me does not only mean having equal portions of work, play and family life. For me, it does not only mean having a sound mind, body and spirit. What I believe is that it is within us to muster the forces of nature to be on our side by reforming our own behavior in order to achieve a well-balanced life. If you do "the right thing", the right thing will come back to you. This is not necessarily karma but the realization that there is positive and negative energy in the universe that is out of our control and beyond our comprehension. Besides gravity and centrifugal force, there are forces in the universe we will never comprehend---frequencies, vibrations, fields of energy, our life force energy that affect people around us. I believe that doing the right thing will harness and call on all these forces to rally behind us. If it won't take too much effort on our part, why not choose to do the right thing? In doing so, I believe we will achieve the unity of mind, body, emotion and spirit which will awaken the genius in us. It is combining the fundamental rules of life with common sense, with the sum of our knowledge and with the unexplainable power of the universe............

Supplemental Disclaimer

The information contained in this book is provided to you "AS IS" and does not constitute legal or financial advice. All sample forms are for educational purposes only. We make no claims, promises or guarantees about the accuracy, completeness, or any specific result from the use of the contents or adequacy of the information contained in this book. Information contained in this book should not be used as substitute for obtaining financial and tax advice from a competent and licensed financial advisor and/or legal advice from an attorney licensed or authorized to practice in your jurisdiction. Medical or health information written in this book must not be misconstrued as medical advice. Consult your doctor or other healthcare provider before acting on any information provided in this book. Narratives in this book are based on true events.

No warranties are made regarding the suitability of this book. This book contains an accumulation of information based on the personal experience of the author. Prior results do not guarantee a similar outcome. The author and publisher do not guarantee the accuracy, completeness, efficacy and timeliness of the information provided herein. The information may no longer be current at the time of publication of this book. The reader should seek the advice of a licensed professional before acting on any information provided herein.

Various advice in this book do not take into account your objectives, financial situation or needs. Before acting on any advice you should consider the appropriateness of the advice and its applicability to your current situation. Any products mentioned in this book may not be appropriate for you. Product Disclosure Statements for those products must be requested and reviewed before making any decisions. We make no claims, promises or guarantees about the accuracy, completeness, or any specific result from the use of the contents or adequacy of the information contained in this book. **Arthur V. Prosper**, its affiliates, parents, subsidiaries, assigns, officers, directors, shareholders, employees, representatives, agents and servants assume no responsibility to any person who relies on information contained herein and disclaim all liability in respect to such information.

PUBLISHER: A-TEAM, LP

DEBT FORGIVENESS Volume 2 WHEN CREDITORS DECIDE TO SUE: Erase Your Credit Card Debts
https://www.amazon.com/DEBT-FORGIVENESS-WHEN-CREDITORS-DECIDE-ebook/dp/B01ACTBTIU/ref=pd sim 351 1? encoding=UTF8&pd rd i=B01ACTBTIU&pd rd r=A001FFR7YYMRE7EEJ7T3&pd rd w=lDdkz&pd rd wg=W1P4U&psc=1&refRID=A001FFR7YYMRE7EEJ7T3

The Simplest Path to Wealth – Turn $50,000 into $3.3 Million
https://www.amazon.com/Simplest-Path-Wealth-Turn-Million-ebook/dp/B01KPQB0OS/ref=asap bc?ie=UTF8

The Six Million Dollar Retiree: Your roadmap to a six million dollar retirement nest egg
https://www.amazon.com/Six-Million-Dollar-Retiree-retirement-ebook/dp/B073XTL47J/ref=sr 1 4?s=digital-text&ie=UTF8&qid=1504026864&sr=1-4&keywords=Arthur V. Prosper

Dynamic Budgeting Techniques: Cut your expenses in half and double your income
https://www.amazon.com/Dynamic-Budgeting-Techniques-expenses-double-ebook/dp/B01LZA9O3W/ref=asap bc?ie=UTF8

Living Rich & Loving It: Your guide to a rich, happy, healthy, simple and balanced life
https://www.amazon.com/Living-Rich-Loving-healthy-balanced-ebook/dp/B01GORIB4Y/ref=sr 1 3?s=digital-text&ie=UTF8&qid=1480539481&sr=1-3&keywords=Arthur V. Prosper

Stop Paying Your Credit Cards: Obtain Credit Card Debt Forgiveness Volume 1
https://www.amazon.com/Stop-Paying-Your-Credit-Cards-ebook/dp/B019ZY3D1E/ref=sr 1 3?s=digital-text&ie=UTF8&qid=1536002927&sr=1-3&keywords=arthur+prosper&dpID=51BYQcDwMKL&preST= SY445 QL70 &dpSrc=srch

Made in the USA
Middletown, DE
13 March 2020